Spiritual Espresso
Volume II

Devotionals from *Strength for Today*

© Copyright 2012 Allen Domelle Ministries
ISBN: 978-0-9833193-3-7
All Scripture quotations are from the King James Bible 1611.
Visit our website at:
oldpathsjournal.com

For more copies:

Allen Domelle Ministries
PO Box 1595
Bethany, OK 73008
903.746.9632

TABLE OF CONTENTS

It's Through the Blood	7
The Importance of Your Appearance	9
The Answer to the World's Problems	11
How to Respond to Fear	13
How to Deal with Disloyalty	15
Action is the Key	17
Rearing Godly Children	19
The Purpose of God's Grace and Mercy	21
So the Wall Was Finished	23
Recipe for Revival	25
Stand for Your Life	27
The Importance of Knowledge	29
Everyone Needs a Daysman	31
When You Are Feeling All Alone	33
Your Spirit Will Tell on You	35
Not for Sale	37
Age Is Not the Measurement of Truth	39
The Result of Seeing God	41
A Hatred of Life	43
Consider	45
The Best of the Best	47
A Formula for God's Blessings	49
Woe Unto Them…	51
His Hand Is Stretched Out Still	53
Is This the Man?	55
A Fading Flower	57
Their Day Is Coming	59
God's Counseling Session	61
Your Central Processing Unit	63
A Portion with the Great	65
Two Requirements for God's Blessings	67

THE BIGNESS OF GOD	69
THE SYMBOL IS NOT GREATER THAN THE OBJECT	71
RESULTS OF COMPLAINING	73
TAKE HEED TO YOURSELVES	75
DON'T HAVE YOUR HAND OUT	77
FINDING GOD IN YOUR LIFE	79
LIVING A LIFE OF SIMPLICITY	81
STOP LYING TO YOURSELF	83
YE HAVE SEEN	85
PLEASANT WORDS	87
ENTERING HIS GATES	89
STAND UPON THY FEET	91
A REMNANT	93
DOTH HE NOT SPEAK PARABLES?	95
WHEN THIS COMETH, YE SHALL KNOW	97
THE RIGHT MINDSET CONCERNING THE MINISTRY	99
CAN THESE BONES LIVE?	101
PROPER DIETARY HABITS ARE BENEFICIAL	103
IN ALL MATTERS OF WISDOM AND UNDERSTANDING	105
STANDING IS NEVER EASY	107
SKILL AND UNDERSTANDING	109
IT'S NOT ALL ABOUT YOU	111
DON'T DESTROY YOUR BROTHER	113
FOOD CONVENIENT FOR ME	115
YOU STILL HAVE GOD	117
ART THOU NOT FROM EVERLASTING?	119
IT SHALL COME TO PASS	121
PAY YOUR DEBT	123
GROW WHERE YOU ARE PLANTED	125
THIRTY PIECES OF SILVER	127
OPENING HEAVEN'S WINDOWS	129
CASTING AND MENDING	131

Are You Worthy?	133
Whom Say Ye That I Am?	135
Actions Speak Louder Than Words	137
This Cup	139
There Cometh One After Me	141
Buildings Are Tools	143
Do You Need a Miracle?	145
Weak Leadership	147
Success Is the Enemy of Success	149
A Proper Perspective	151
Dealing with the Lost	153
He Came to Us	155
Hear Counsel	157
Opening Your Understanding	159
Do You Believe God's Word?	161
Walk in the Day	163
Much Fruit	165
Do You Really Know Them?	167
What He Really Said Was…	169
Watch Yourself When You Disagree	171
The Most Important Duties of the Church	173
How to Settle Religious Questions	175
Watch and Remember	177
For What Are You Known?	179
Don't Be a Know-It-All	181
Sin's Lie	183
Getting Along with People	185
Signs of Carnality	187
Knowledge Versus Charity	189
Charity Has a Blind Eye	191
You're Not Alone	193
The Purpose of a Thorn in the Flesh	195

ARE YOU FILLED WITH THE SPIRIT?	197
PLEASE BE PATIENT	199
GOD'S WILL FOR YOU	201
FIRST OF ALL	203
OVERCOMING FEAR	205
THERE REMAINETH A REST FOR THE PEOPLE OF GOD	207
CAN THEY DEPEND UPON YOU?	209
PRACTICING PURE RELIGION	211
ADVICE FOR YOUR MARRIAGE	213
BUILDING YOUR FAITH	215
WHAT CAN WASH AWAY MY SIN?	217
DO YOU WANT A PROMOTION?	219
QUESTIONS VERSUS ABSOLUTES	221
THANK GOD FOR THE WORD "IS."	223

It's Through the Blood

2 Chronicles 3:14
"And he made the vail of blue, and purple, and crimson, and fine linen, and wrought cherubims thereon."

As God went through the building of the temple, He described for us each different piece of furniture and the separation of the rooms. In this temple, there were two rooms separated by a vail. These rooms were the Holy Place and the Holy of Holies. The vail was a curtain that was blue, purple and crimson. I believe God made the vail these colors to remind us that the only way we can have fellowship with the King of kings, Who is Jehovah God, is through the blood of Christ. Let me explain the meaning of the colors.

The first color we see is blue. Blue is a type of Heaven. Heaven is where God lives and is where He will take us some day if we are saved. The second color is purple. Purple in the Bible is a color of royalty. Yes, God is royalty! He is the King of kings. He alone will sit on the throne in Heaven. Then God puts a third color on this vail, the color crimson. Crimson is red and is a type of the blood of Christ. Each of these colors together reminds us of salvation. Let me explain.

God is in Heaven, and He sits upon His throne as King of kings. The vail separates us from having fellowship personally with Him. The only way this vail can be torn down so we can have access to Him is through the blood of Jesus Christ. When Jesus died, the Bible states that the vail was *"rent in twain."* It was Jesus' blood that allowed us into the Holy of Holies. Without the blood of Christ, we cannot have fellowship with God and we cannot go to Heaven.

This is why we must understand that nothing other than the blood of Jesus Christ can take us to Heaven; not our church, or our works, or our goodness, or our religion or even a spiritual leader. Only the blood of Jesus can take us to Heaven. If there has never been a time in your life when you accepted the blood of Jesus as the payment for your sins, then you cannot go to Heaven.

I ask you to be sure you have accepted Jesus and Jesus alone as your only way to Heaven. Put your trust in Him and He will save you. If for some reason you are not sure how to do this or have some question, please feel free to contact me so that I can show you from the Bible how you can be saved and make Heaven your final destination when you die.

The Importance of Your Appearance

2 Chronicles 9:3-4
"And when the queen of Sheba had seen the wisdom of Solomon, and the house that he had built, And the meat of his table, and the sitting of his servants, and the attendance of his ministers, and their apparel; his cupbearers also, and their apparel; and his ascent by which he went up into the house of the LORD; there was no more spirit in her."

We hear the statement quite often, "The cover sells the book." This statement is truer than what most people realize. Not only does the cover sell the book, but the appearance sells the life.

In the story of Solomon and the queen of Sheba, we read that she did not believe all the stories that people had told her about Solomon and the greatness of his kingdom. Because of this, she came to see for herself if all that she heard was true. As she came, she had prepared some questions that would test his wisdom and, to her amazement, he had an answer for everything she asked. What I want you to notice is that there was something else that really sold her about all the stories that she had heard. It was the appearance. How his servants conducted themselves and how they dressed left her in amazement, for the appearance portrayed what was in the hearts of Solomon and his servants.

In this generation, we have really thrown this principle out the window. We live in the sloppiest generation that I can remember. I am one of those who believe your appearance tells a lot about you. This is why I believe that no matter where we go, we ought to have on our best appearance. Not just in action, but also in our clothing. Yes, I do believe we ought to have the right appearance in our actions. God's people should be happy, and God's people should put on an appearance of what is going on in our hearts.

What I really would like to see from the readers of this devotional is for you to have on your best appearance in your clothing at all times. Stop being so sloppy. You must understand that everywhere you go you represent Jesus Christ. This should motivate you to dress sharp all of the time. I am not saying that we have to have the most expensive clothing, but I am a believer in dressing sharp and dressing for the occasion no matter where you go. In other words, some need to simply iron their clothes. Others need to stop being casual all of the time. Whatever happened to people dressing sharp even in their casual wear?

I fly somewhere almost every week. I am amazed at how sloppy people dress to fly in airplanes. Quite often I receive compliments from the stewardess about how sharply I am dressed. I believe this is only because most people just don't dress up to fly any more.

Christian, when you go to church make sure your appearance is what it ought to be. When you go to a restaurant, make sure your appearance is what it ought to be. Wherever you go, make sure your appearance is sharp because the world is watching us and we should want to put on a good appearance for our Saviour no matter where we are. Realize the world is watching us and our appearance tells a lot about what we are. Let us sell to the world that what we have is important by making sure we are dressed appropriately at all times. Realize that as the cover sells the book, so also will your appearance sell to the world what you have is real. Let us be a people who, at all times, have the right appearance.

The Answer to the World's Problems

2 Chronicles 15:2
"And he went out to meet Asa, and said unto him, Hear ye me, Asa, and all Judah and Benjamin; The LORD is with you, while ye be with him; and if ye seek him, he will be found of you; but if ye forsake him, he will forsake you."

Asa had seen some great success in his kingdom for some time. Asa, after becoming king of Judah, immediately took away the strange gods of the land and removed their altars and the groves where these altars were set up. Because of this, Asa had seen the blessings of God upon his leadership in a great way. He saw God help him in the conquering of the Ethiopian army because he cried unto God for His help.

Now God came to Asa through the Prophet Azariah to remind him that as long as he would seek the LORD that the LORD would be with him and bless him and his kingdom. However, he was also reminded that the very moment he forsook the LORD that the LORD would also forsake him and that his kingdom would see hardships because of his actions. In the latter part of chapter 16 we see that this is the very thing that happened. In his pride, Asa stopped relying upon the LORD and began to rely upon man. This action caused the LORD to send upon him a disease that followed him to his grave. You see, this verse was a reminder that the blessings upon a nation are reliant upon whether or not a nation seeks after the LORD.

As I write this devotional, the world is seemingly in great financial turmoil. Yesterday alone the Dow Jones dropped over 600 points to the lowest point it has been in five years. We have seen several bank failures in the United States and see the world's economy tanking. All of this is happening and people are nervous about their future. In the mean time, we see the political figures scrambling to find the answer to turn this around. They have come up with loaning billions of dollars to help these troubled banks recover. They have sent out stimulus checks to their citizens hoping to boost the economy. They have grappled over what to do and yet seem to miss the answer to this world's problem.

The answer to the problems we are facing in the world right now is found in 2 Chronicles 15:2. The answer is getting back to seeking the LORD. We live in a society that has forsaken the LORD and because of this, the LORD has forsaken us. The only answer to this world's problems is for this world to start seeking the LORD again.

Now you may wonder what this has to do with you. Let me tell you what it has to do with you. This world is made up of people, and you are a part of this world. This means if the world is going to start seeking the LORD then it starts with individuals seeking the LORD. That means you and I must seek the LORD in order to get God's blessings upon our lives. Whether or not the world seeks God should not stop us from seeking Him. God's blessings can be upon our lives if we will seek Him.

So, as you go throughout your day today, don't forget to seek the LORD. In everything you do, seek the LORD and His wisdom. Ask Him what you should do and do it. In so doing, we as individuals can start to bring the blessings of God back upon our nation and our world.

How to Respond to Fear

2 Chronicles 20:3
"And Jehoshaphat feared, and set himself to seek the LORD, and proclaimed a fast throughout all Judah."

Fear is a horrible thing that many people face in life. The presence of fear causes people to respond in bad ways. The 1828 Webster dictionary says, "fear is an uneasiness of mind, upon the thought of future evil likely to befall us."

We must acknowledge that fear is a part of life. However, we also must realize that fear does not come from God. According to 2 Timothy 1:7, God is not the one who gave us fear. So, if fear is not of God then fear must come from the Devil. Let's face it, with the turmoil that our world is in, it is an easy thing to have fear. If we are going to overcome fear, we need the proper response to fear. Let me explain what the proper response to fear should be when it comes in your life.

We learn in 2 Chronicles 20:3 that Jehoshaphat had fear. As you read through the whole chapter, you will learn how you ought to respond to fear in order to get God to step in to help you. Notice first of all, the proper response when fear comes is to seek the LORD. It did not say when fear comes you should run. No, running is exactly what Satan would want you to do. God wants you to face your fears, but He also does not want you to face your fears alone. God wants to face your fears with you and this is why your first response to fear should be to seek the LORD.

Second, in verse 4, we learn our response to fear after our initial step of seeking God is to ask God for His help. When fear comes your way, the only One who can truly help you is God. This is why you must ask God for His help and not man. What can man do with your fears? Only God can help you with the fears you face in life. So, because God is the only One Who can help you, ask Him for His help.

Third, after you have asked God for His help then you need to take some time and remember the power of God by remembering His great works in the past. Notice in verses 6 and 7 that Jehoshaphat began to remind himself and the people of God's great power by reminding them what God had done for them in the past. When fear comes your way, you must take time to remember the great works of God for He is the One from Whom you are asking help.

Fourth, when fear comes, tell God your situation and that of which you are afraid. In verse 10, Jehoshaphat not only told God their situation, but he also reminded God of what he feared. Let me just say, there is nothing wrong with admitting to God that you are afraid. When fear has gripped your heart, acknowledge to God what your fears are. Tell God your situation, and be honest with Him telling Him your fears about the situation you face. He wants to know how you feel and He wants you to pour your heart out to Him.

Last, when fear comes, acknowledge your helplessness to God. This is truly why we have fear anyway. Fear comes when we feel helpless with our situation. When fear comes, acknowledge to God your helplessness and your need to have Him intercede.

Yes, fear is a part of life and everyone will face fear at sometime in their life. So whatever you are fearful of today, take the Bible formula and apply it. Like Jehoshaphat did, if you will apply this formula to your life when fear comes, God will step in and help you with your fear. Let us remember that fear is not of God, but when fear does come, God is the only One Who can help you with your fears.

How to Deal with Disloyalty

2 Chronicles 23:15
"So they laid hands on her; and when she was come to the entering of the horse gate by the king's house, they slew her there."

Disloyalty must be dealt with swiftly and properly. Disloyalty is a terrible sin and an evil sin; evil because it hurts others who are influenced by the disloyalty. We learn in this verse how to deal with those who are disloyal.

First of all, you must deal with disloyalty openly. It must be dealt with openly because the disloyalty was expressed openly. Normally I tell people never to deal with sin in an open manner because it will cause you to rarely recover the one who has committed the sin. However, because disloyalty is expressed openly, then you must deal with it openly so everyone can see what happens when one is disloyal.

Second, you must deal with disloyalty quickly. The longer you let disloyalty go unpunished the more that disloyalty will hurt leadership and the unity of the team, church, or organization. As uncomfortable as it may be to deal with disloyalty, you must quickly deal with it for it will not settle itself. The longer you let disloyal people perform their disloyal ways the more that disloyalty will affect others.

Last, you must completely squelch all disloyalty. We see in this story that disloyalty was dealt with by death. Now it is not our place to take the punishment to this extreme. In this case, this was the proper punishment, but in most cases you must deal with disloyalty by getting rid of the person who is disloyal. You must not and you cannot allow a disloyal person to continue to have the privilege of being a part of the organization. Disloyalty demands that the person who is disloyal never be allowed to be a part of the team, the organization or the group of people about which the disloyalty is being expressed. Let me warn you of a couple of things concerning disloyalty.

First of all, don't you ever be guilty of disloyalty on the job, in the church, on a team, in the school or in any other organization with which you are involved. Disloyalty is an evil sin and you must not allow yourself to be involved in this evil.

Second, parents do not allow your children to practice disloyalty. When you see a child being disloyal, you must quickly punish them in the proper manner according to what the Bible teaches. If you let them get by with disloyalty, then you just may allow them to destroy their life.

Last, to the employer, you also cannot allow disloyalty on the job. When you find an employee being disloyal, you must let them go. You cannot allow disloyalty in the work place for this will destroy the morale of the work place and will affect the quality of the work that is to be done.

Let us all guard ourselves from disloyalty. Don't ever find yourself being a part of disloyalty. If you have been disloyal, then be sure to get this right with God and with everyone to whom you have expressed your disloyalty.

Action is the Key

Proverbs 13:4
"The soul of the sluggard desireth, and hath nothing: but the soul of the diligent shall be made fat."

As the father in the book of Proverbs instructed the son, he taught him the difference between the sluggard and the diligent. According to the 1828 Webster's dictionary, we find that a sluggard is one who is "habitually lazy, idle and inactive." On the other hand Webster defines the diligent as "attentive; industrious; not idle or negligent." In this verse we find quite a contrast between the two types of people.

As I study this verse, I see, on the surface, both the sluggard and the diligent seem to be the same with one main difference between the two. First of all, you will see that both the sluggard and the diligent have desire. Desire is certainly a good quality for a person to have. In fact, a person without desire is certain to go nowhere in life real fast. Desire comes from a wish or a passion to have something. So this would mean if a person has desire, they probably have dreams as well. As you can see, the sluggard and the diligent both seem to have dreams which lead to desire.

The big difference between the diligent and the sluggard is what they do with their desire. The difference between the two is action. Action is the key that defines the difference between the two. It is fine to have dreams and it is fine to have desire, but without action, your desires will leave you empty.

Yes, there is risk in action, but the benefits of the action far outweigh the benefits of inaction. Notice, the sluggard without acting upon his desire has nothing; whereas, the diligent acting upon his desire, is made fat with the accomplishment of what he set out to do.

We must ask ourselves, which category do we fall into? Do you find yourself desiring, but always have an excuse as to why you don't act on your desire? God says this type of person is a sluggard, and certainly, you would not want to fall into this category. I implore you to take action on your desires. You will never get anywhere without acting upon your desires. Yes, there will be risk in your quest to acquire your desire, but you are sure to get nothing if you don't set out with action.

Every parent needs to take time to teach their children the principle this father was teaching his son. Don't be guilty of doing things for your children all the time. Make them take action if they want something. Make them figure out a way to get what they desire. In so doing, you will teach them to become a diligent person in life who does not depend upon others to give things to them.

Of course the best way for us to teach our children diligence is to be diligent ourselves. Be careful about always having excuses as to why you don't or can't pursue your desires. Lay aside your excuses and take action today towards the desires that you have; especially the desires which God has placed in your heart.

Rearing Godly Children

2 Chronicles 34:3
"For in the eighth year of his reign, while he was yet young, he began to seek after the God of David his father: and in the twelfth year he began to purge Judah and Jerusalem from the high places, and the groves, and the carved images, and the molten images."

As far as I know, I have never found a person who is truly an expert on rearing children. If there was a fail safe book that could make children turn out right, I would imagine that it would be the best seller for many years. The reason there is no book like this is because every child has their own will, and because they have their own will, they will ultimately determine their own course of life. As parents all we can do is our best to guide them down the right path of life so they have a better chance to make the right decisions for their life.

In the verse that we just read, we see Josiah was a young person who began to seek God. I am encouraged to see that we don't have to wait until a person becomes an adult to get them to serve God. Serving God should always start in childhood. According to this verse, Josiah was sixteen years old when he began to seek after God's will. This probably means that he had some influence that helped him seek after God when he was younger, for one does not suddenly start seeking God without having some prior guidance to do so. I believe we can learn something from the life of Josiah that will help us in rearing godly children, and that is to start training them while they are young to serve God. In doing so, we have a better chance of our children serving God when they come of age to make the right decisions. Let me give you a few thoughts that I believe will help our children turn out right.

First of all, don't give your children a choice in doing right. One of the greatest mistakes I hear of in our society today is parents saying they don't want to force their children to go to church or to do right. Now this is crazy to say at the least! Do you give your children a choice on whether or not to do drugs? Of course not! So why would you give them the choice of doing right? Your job as a parent is to help your children to make the right decisions. Stop giving your children a choice about doing right, and lead them in doing right.

Second, make sure your children are faithful to every church service. Again, don't give your children a choice in this matter. My parents never gave me a choice when it came to going to church. They just said, "It is church time," and we went to church. If you want your children to seek God when they are older, then create a habit in them of going to church when they are young.

Third, make sure they read the Bible and pray every day. As a parent you need to make sure they spend some time reading the Bible and praying daily. This time does not have to be lengthy, but they should spend some time reading the Bible and praying.

Fourth, help them to choose the right friends. Don't give them a choice in their friends. If you see one of their friends who you do not think is a good influence, then tell them to stop spending time with that child. Teach them they don't have to be rude to them; they just need to stop spending time with them.

Last, be an example yourself of doing right. Nothing will create a desire in your children to do right more than mom and dad doing right. Our lives are the greatest example from which our children can learn.

Again, I am no expert on child rearing. I can only hope my daughter turns out right. However, I can do everything in my power to make sure she turns out right. Be the leader you are supposed to be, and lead your children to make the right decisions of life. In doing so, you have a better chance of them serving God when they are older.

The Purpose of God's Grace and Mercy

Ezra 9:8-9
"And now for a little space grace hath been shewed from the LORD our God, to leave us a remnant to escape, and to give us a nail in his holy place, that our God may lighten our eyes, and give us a little reviving in our bondage. For we were bondmen; yet our God hath not forsaken us in our bondage, but hath extended mercy unto us in the sight of the kings of Persia, to give us a reviving, to set up the house of our God, and to repair the desolations thereof, and to give us a wall in Judah and in Jerusalem."

Why would God give us grace and mercy? What is the purpose or why would God have mercy on people such as us and even show grace to us? We find the answer in these two verses.

Ezra, after the rebuilding of the temple and returning to his position of service to the king, came back to the land to see what the people had done. When he came back, he saw the people living the very same lifestyle that brought God's judgment upon them. Because of this, he went to God and prayed a prayer which we read here in chapter 9 of Ezra. In this prayer, Ezra makes a statement of why God extends to us His grace and shows mercy upon us. The purpose, he says, is *"to give us a reviving."* The whole purpose why God showed His grace to His people is to give them a chance to come back to Him.

God is a just God and He must judge sin, but God would much rather give us a chance to get right so He can bless us. Each of us should realize that God's grace and mercy are not a license to sin. Instead, His grace and mercy are an opportunity to get right with Him so we do not have to face His judgment. This is why we read in the Bible that salvation is offered to us by God's grace. We do not deserve salvation, but it is an act of God's grace that He offers it to us. This grace should not be wasted, and each person should take the opportunity of God's grace to accept salvation through Jesus Christ.

Let me take this one step further. Everyday of our lives God shows us grace and mercy. There are many of us, if not all of us, whom God could show His wrath upon because of our sin. We must be careful that we don't waste the opportunity of God's grace and mercy. We should use this opportunity to make sure we are right with God.

Let's bring this down to a very personal level; are you wasting the grace and mercy of God in your life? We all deserve the judgment of God upon our lives. There are none of us who are perfect. Daily we must be sure that we don't waste the grace and mercy that God extends to us. Have you had a personal revival lately in your life because of the grace and mercy that God has given to you? Or, have you wasted His grace and mercy by continuing on in the same old lifestyle that will bring His wrath upon you? Today, let each of us take inventory of our spiritual lives. Be sure that in the areas where God has shown you His grace and mercy that you don't waste those times, but use them for the purpose for which God extended them to you. Remember, that purpose is *"to give us a reviving."* Let's have a personal revival today and use the grace and mercy of God for the purpose for which He has given them to us.

So the Wall Was Finished

Nehemiah 6:15
"So the wall was finished in the twenty and fifth day of the month Elul, in fifty and two days."

Nehemiah came to the city of Jerusalem and saw the walls of the city in disrepair. His burden for his city motivated him to repair the walls of the city back to their former condition. This verse states that in fifty-two days they repaired these walls. What a great task this was for Nehemiah. So, we must keep in mind that all the events from chapters 3 through 6 happened in fifty-two days. What a great accomplishment these people made in such a short amount of time.

What I want you to notice in this verse is the phrase, *"So the wall was finished…"* It is a great statement for anyone to be able to say that they finished what they started. Yes, there were a lot of things that could have stopped them during this time, but they kept on working until the wall was finished. These people were not just busy, but they were working until they finished what they started.

I remember years ago, I heard a secretary from a large church say about her pastor and boss that he did not care how many hours they worked as long as they were accomplishing something everyday. She continued on by saying that there are many people who are busy for many hours a day who do not accomplish anything during those hours. She finished by saying, work is accomplishing something. She made the statement that you have not really worked until you have accomplished or finished something. What a powerful statement!

I believe what she said is very true. As I travel weekly holding revival meetings, I hear the schedule of pastors and assistant pastors and am amazed that there is not more being done. You see, work is accomplishing something. You may stay busy throughout the day, but are you truly working? You may actually stay busy for ten to twelve hours a day, but at the end of the day what have you accomplished? If you have not accomplished something in that day, you have not really worked.

Be careful that you don't become the type of person who stays busy but does not accomplish things. I am not at all saying a person who does not accomplish something is lazy. I am saying that every day you need to be able to go home and say I accomplished something at work today.

Parents, be careful to teach your children the difference between staying busy and accomplishing something. You need to make sure that you give your children something to accomplish every day. Don't let them finish a day without accomplishing something. When they do accomplish something, point it out to them and praise them for finishing a job. Accomplishing a job brings fulfillment to a person's life because they finished something.

As you go throughout the day, be sure that you accomplish something. At the end of every day you need to ask yourself this question, "What have I accomplished today?" If you didn't accomplish anything then be sure to accomplish something tomorrow. At the end of every day, you should have a list of things you have accomplished. Don't be a person who is busy but never accomplishes anything. Be a person who, at the end of every day, can look at a list of things you have accomplished and with Nehemiah say, *"So the...was finished."*

Recipe for Revival

Nehemiah 8:6
"And Ezra blessed the LORD, the great God. And all the people answered, Amen, Amen, with lifting up their hands: and they bowed their heads, and worshipped the LORD with their faces to the ground."

In the eighth chapter of the book of Nehemiah, a revival took place among the remnant of Israel. You will see in this chapter the recipe they followed in order to have revival. Today our nation needs to have revival! The need for revival is great, and if we will follow the recipe for revival that we see in this chapter, we also can have revival today. Let me take you through what it took for them to have revival.

First of all, in verse one, we see the people had one heart for revival. If revival is ever going to take place, then people must desire with their whole heart to have a revival. You cannot have a divided heart that says, "I want revival," and then in the next breath want and live for something else. The need for revival in our nations, churches and our personal lives must consume us if we are ever going to have revival.

Second, no revival has ever taken place without the Bible. Notice in verses one and two that they brought the Book of the Law. You will never have revival without the Bible being read. It is the Bible that convicts us of sin. It is the Bible that shows our wickedness. You will never have revival in your personal life without reading the Bible. Too many times we say we want revival, but we never read the Bible in order to have revival.

Third, revival will come when there is preaching. In verses seven and eight, we see the Bible was read and explained *"distinctly"* to the people so they could understand what It says. Practical, precise and clear preaching is what it takes for people to have revival. Our land will never have revival until the pulpits of our churches become red-hot with preaching.

As long as we have feel-good preaching, our churches and lives will continue to be cold and indifferent. Feel-good preaching has never brought revival. It has always been the pointed, clear, easy to understand and honest preaching that has brought revival. If you want a personal revival or a revival in your church, then you must get back to preaching that, in a very clear and pointed way, tells you what you are doing wrong.

Fourth, revival comes when there is a repentant heart. In verse nine, we see them weeping because of what the Bible showed them about their sins. Revival will never happen until we repent of the sins that we have committed. I am talking about using the altars once again in our churches. As long as the altars are empty, the revival fires will not burn. As long as you personally stay in your pew and do not use the altar to repent of your sins, you will not have personal revival.

Last, once revival has come, it takes a continual maintenance of daily confessing our sins to keep the revival going. You will notice in chapter nine and verse two that the people continued to confess their sins. Once revival has come in your life, if you want it to continue, then you must keep your heart and life clear of sin by daily confessing sin and daily getting right with God.

Oh, how we need revival! Revival in a nation will only happen when we as individuals have personal revival. Do you need a revival in your life? Can you honestly say that everything is clear between you and God? Today, take this recipe for revival and start applying it and ask God to give you a revival. When each individual starts having revival, a nation will have revival. National revivals only happen when individuals have revival.

Stand for Your Life

Esther 8:11
"Wherein the king granted the Jews which were in every city to gather themselves together, and to stand for their life, to destroy, to slay, and to cause to perish, all the power of the people and province that would assault them, both little ones and women, and to take the spoil of them for a prey,"

We live in a very passive society today. It is very disturbing to see people so passive about issues that could destroy our nation and our fundamental movement as we know it.

In the days in which this story was written, it seemed the Jews were very passive about everything that was going on in their kingdom. Many things probably contributed to this attitude. Their defeat and the captivity in which they were currently living was certainly one of the causes. The hate for the nation in which they lived was probably another cause. Maybe the biggest cause was the mentality that whatever they did would not affect anything anyway. Regardless, whatever the reason, now their lives were at stake.

A law had been given to destroy all the Jews. Mordecai sent a post to all the Jews and begged them to *"stand for their life."* He begged them because their future was at stake, and if there were ever a time to stand, this was that time. Because they would not stand for any other reason, Mordecai told them to at least stand for their life's sake.

There are many reasons for which people should stand up and fight. I believe we should stand for right and against wrong. However, to be quite honest with you, it seems we live in a society that seems to be very passive about the change that is going on in our nation and in present-day fundamentalism. As people are passive about the issues going on today, the crowd who wants to destroy us is certainly accomplishing their agenda. Their agenda is to change our nation and fundamentalism as we know it.

I come to you today and say it is time we stand for our life. If we are not willing to stand for any other reason, we need to stand for the sake of our life; our future. Standing means we will do what it takes to get our agenda done even if it means we will lose friends and influence over our stance. It takes character to do this! Yet, we need people today to stand for their life. You may not have a public pulpit where many can hear you, but it takes everybody doing right to affect change.

I come to the Christian and say, stand for your life. When you see the main movement in fundamentalism changing the Word of God and what we believe about It, stand up and say you will not be a part of it. When you see Christianity becoming more like the world, don't change to be like everyone else. Stand up for your life! When you see the country in which you live continually move to the left, stand for right even if it seems as if your stance will not change anything. We cannot and must not be passive about the changes we see going on in our nation and in the movement of fundamentalism. We must stand for our life's sake.

I ask you, are you standing for right when you see changes going on or are you the one who sits quietly by because you don't want to upset the apple cart? It is those who quietly sit by and don't say anything even when they see things which shouldn't be happening, who are the cause of compromise and societal changes. I beg of you today, stand for your life, for not only is your future at stake, but the future of your children is at stake as well.

The Importance of Knowledge

Proverbs 19:2
"Also, that the soul be without knowledge, it is not good; and he that hasteth with his feet sinneth."

God warns us in this verse about what the lack of knowledge does. He shows us that the lack of knowledge will cause a man to make hasty decisions which always lead to heartache and trouble. God says that it is not good for a person to be without knowledge. An analogy of what God is saying here is: it is not good to work with electricity with wet hands. Another analogy is that it is never good to touch a hot stove. Now I know this seems very simple and common, but that is exactly what God wants us to understand. He wants us to understand how bad it is to go through life without knowledge. If the lack of knowledge causes me to make hurtful hasty decisions, then I would be wise to live life trying to acquire knowledge.

Knowledge makes us aware of things so that we don't perform actions that could hurt us. God wants us to be aware of the dangers ahead and this awareness can only come through having knowledge. So how do we get knowledge?

First of all, you get knowledge through reading the Bible. The Bible is the source of all knowledge because the Bible is the Word of God. Who better to receive knowledge from than the source of all knowledge; God? I always like going to a source to get something, for the source always gives you what you want in its purest form. If you want knowledge, you should spend time daily in the Bible, for the Bible will give you knowledge in its purest form. The Bible will give you the knowledge of God.

Second, we can get knowledge from counsel. I believe that, if you want knowledge in life, you would be very wise to get counsel from your parents, pastor or spiritual leaders about what you ought to do in life. Far too many times people let their pride keep them from getting counsel. Remember, it is not good for the soul to be without knowledge. So, if it is not good to be without knowledge, you would be wise to swallow your pride and get counsel about decisions and endeavors you want to pursue in life.

Third, you can get knowledge from letting people teach you. I have always been taught that everybody is my teacher. Everybody can teach me something that I do not know. Learn to be observant of people and learn from them. Remember, you learn more from listening than you do from talking. Don't be a know-it-all type of person and let people teach you the knowledge that they have. When people try to teach you something, don't always come back with something better to show them your knowledge. If you want knowledge, you must let others teach you.

Last of all, you can get knowledge by reading books. Maybe one of the biggest sins in our generation is that people don't read anymore. Reading will give you knowledge. When is the last time you read a book? If I want knowledge, I will read the right type of books in order to gain knowledge. If I read a whole book and just gain one piece of knowledge, then the reading of that book was worth it all. Turn off your TV and computer and grab a book to read so you can gain some knowledge.

Remember, God warns us that being without knowledge is not good. Don't be guilty of being a person without knowledge. Take this counsel given in this devotional and make it a habit to learn something everyday. Don't end the day without learning a new piece of knowledge.

Everyone Needs a Daysman

Job 9:33
"Neither is there any daysman betwixt us, that might lay his hand upon us both."

Job 13:19
"Who is he that will plead with me? for now, if I hold my tongue, I shall give up the ghost."

In Job's defense against the accusations of his friends, he makes two statements that should make every Christian realize the importance of praying for others. He makes a statement in Job 9:33, *"Neither is there any daysman betwixt us."* Then again in Job 13:19 he says, *"Who is he that will plead with me?"* Job in these verses was literally begging for someone to intercede for him.

The word *"daysman"* means "an umpire" or "an arbiter" or "a mediator." What a powerful word! Job needed someone to be his daysman. He was saying he needed someone who would stand for him in prayer to God instead of someone trying to tell him what he had done wrong. Yes, every person needs a daysman. Every person needs someone who will be their umpire to God. Every person needs someone who will arbitrate their cause to God. Every person needs someone who will stand between them and God for their cause.

I ask you, have you prayed for someone today? Let me be very honest with you, if your prayer life is all about you, then you have a very shallow prayer life. I have no problem with people praying to God for their needs for God commands us to do so. However, there needs to be people that will be a daysman for others and plead to God for the cause of others.

Do you understand the power that a daysman has? If a daysman has the power of an umpire, an arbiter or a mediator, then once a decision has been made, it is final. In other words, God is saying that when you pray for someone else as their daysman, your prayer can have the powerful effect of finalizing God's decision regarding their situation. God is literally teaching us that we can be the deciding factor of whether or not someone has their cause met with God. How terrible it would be if because of our selfish prayer life, the needs of others would not be met.

Today, and every day, find the needs of others and be a daysman to God for them. Pray for others needs the way you would want others to pray for your needs. If you learned to pray for others, imagine how much more power you could have in your prayer life. Let us make sure that those who know us could never say that they did not have a daysman to plead for them. Let us be sure that those who are our acquaintances have a daysman to stand for them in prayer. Let each of us become a person who prays and pleads for the cause of others. I simply ask you this question, who have you prayed for today?

When You Are Feeling All Alone

Job 19:13
"He hath put my brethren far from me, and mine acquaintance are verily estranged from me."

As Job goes through this great trial in his life, we see in this chapter the loneliness that he was experiencing. It seemed to him that he was all alone. Imagine, his children were gone, his wife had just about forsaken him, his so-called friends were criticizing him, his employees had all been killed and it seemed to him that God was nowhere to be seen. What a lonely time he seemed to be going through in his life.

Loneliness is a horrible feeling. I travel quite often and there are times in my travels, as I am alone in a hotel room or sitting on a plane, when loneliness can certainly creep in. There are several reasons why a person can be lonely. It could be a job which requires you to travel alone quite often. It could be that you feel you have no friends. It could be your spouse has either left you or has gone on to Heaven. It could be that you are the last remaining sibling alive in your family. It could be that you sit in a prison cell. It could be that you are a missionary several thousand miles away from home. It could be that you are in the military stationed away from home. It could be several reasons which I have not mentioned. Loneliness is a fact of life that we all must deal with at some time. If we don't deal with loneliness in the right way, then loneliness can certainly cause us to have a negative spirit. Let me show you several ways to deal with loneliness.

First of all, remember God is alive. Notice in verse twenty-five of this chapter that Job said his *"redeemer liveth."* When loneliness comes your way, for whatever reason, you must remember that God is still alive. In other words, I am saying to look to God instead of looking at yourself when loneliness comes. God is the only One Who can help you in your loneliness.

Second, remember you are saved. In verse twenty-five, Job said his *"redeemer"* was alive. If you are saved, you must realize that your Redeemer is Jesus Christ and He is alive and well. Because He is your Redeemer, this means you are saved. Hey, you want to encourage yourself in times of loneliness, just remind yourself that you are saved and will never go to Hell!

Third, remember that one day you will stand with Christ. We see in verse twenty-five that one day Christ will stand upon the Earth. If Christ will stand upon the Earth, this means we will stand with Him. This means that loneliness will not be forever.

Fourth, in times of loneliness, remember your destination. In verse twenty-six, Job reminded himself that he would one day be in Heaven. Nothing will help you more than realizing that you are headed to a place where you will never be alone again. That place is Heaven! You may be alone today, but if you are saved, your loneliness is only temporary.

Last, remember that God will never leave you. In Hebrews 13:5, we are promised that God will never leave us. You may feel that you are alone, but let me promise you, you are never alone. God is with you even during those times when you feel all alone.

So, whatever the cause of your loneliness, always remember these steps that I mentioned and you will find that your loneliness does not have to be as hard as it is for you right now. Keep your eyes on God, for He is always with you and you will never again have to feel that you are alone.

Your Spirit Will Tell on You

Proverbs 20:27
"The spirit of man is the candle of the LORD, searching all the inward parts of the belly."

This verse reminds me of home when I was a boy. We would keep candles in a certain place of our house just in case the power went out. Whenever the power would go out in the house, we would get in the cabinets where we kept the candles, and light them, so we could have light in the house. I believe God is trying to show us that this is what our spirit is to our life.

In the Bible, when you see the word *"spirit"* with the letter "s" in lowercase, it is normally talking about the attitude or disposition of a person. In other words, when God talks about the spirit of a man, He is talking about the attitude of a man, or the disposition of a man, or even the outlook a man has on life. God says that the spirit of man is like a candle and it shows us what kind of person you truly are. In other words, your spirit tells on you. You may think that you can hide what you are on the inside, but your spirit will tell others what kind of person you are.

For instance, a person with a bad attitude has issues in their life that they need to solve. This is why we can tell if a teenager is rebellious or not by their attitude or their spirit. What happens is their spirit or attitude is simply showing others what is going on inside of them. Now we may not like this, but this means we better be careful what type of spirit we have every day. Our spirit is telling a story about us to others.

Now if you don't like the story your spirit is telling others about you, then you would be wise to change your spirit. Truthfully though, the only way to change your spirit is to change who you are on the inside. You will never change your spirit until you change who you truly are. You can only put on an act for so long, and then eventually, the true person will come out in your spirit.

I ask you this question, if I were to go to your workplace, what story would they tell me about you based on your spirit? If I were to go to your house and ask your family members about your spirit, what story would they tell me about you? If I went to your church and asked the members of your church about you, what story would they be reading by your spirit? Do they read that you are obstinate because you are always bucking the system? Do they read that you are backslidden because you never respond during the preaching or invitation? What story would they be telling me about you because of your spirit?

How careful we all must be in what we display through our spirit. Your spirit will tell the story of what you are on the inside, so be careful about the story you tell.

Not for Sale

Proverbs 23:23
"Buy the truth, and sell it not; also wisdom, and instruction, and understanding."

There are some things in life that should never be for sale. Some things that we get are just too valuable for a price tag. I can remember talking to a man years ago who made the statement to me, "Everything is for sale for the right price." Now that may sound good, but the truth is there are some things, no matter what is offered, we should never sell.

God tells us four things in this verse that we should never sell. God says truth, wisdom, instruction and understanding are never to be sold. In other words, God was saying there should never be a price tag on giving these things up. These things are too valuable to be sold. When you learn these things, you should never give them up.

I say this because I look at America and at fundamentalism and wonder why we are so willing to give up the truth that we have learned from the past. America has become a nation of political correctness. America has sold the truth of what we have learned from history for the pleasures of today's lifestyles. I have seen our independent Baptist movement forsake the truth for the sake of being more acceptable in the eyes of Christendom. What a travesty it is to sell the truth and forsake the wisdom and instruction of those from the past.

Let us be careful not to forsake what we have been taught by those in the past. Instead of looking ahead to find out where we should go, we should look to the past to find out where we should go. America would be wise to look to the past generations to find out where we should go instead of being so wrapped up in change. Likewise, fundamentalism should look to the past men of God to decide what we believe in instead of looking to modern day Evangelicalism. Listen, we have the truth, don't sell it!

I ask you, what is the price tag you have put on what you have learned from the past? For what are you willing to trade the principles of the past? Are you willing to sell the truth of the past for convenience, money, position or fame? Don't ever sell truth for anything! For once we have sold truth, then all we have are lies. Protect it and live by it!.

Age Is Not the Measurement of Truth

Job 32:6-7
"And Elihu the son of Barachel the Buzite answered and said, I am young, and ye are very old; wherefore I was afraid, and durst not shew you mine opinion. I said, Days should speak, and multitude of years should teach wisdom."

Recently I was listening to a sermon by a preacher who was trying to defend his position on a subject by using his age as his defense. As I listened to this sermon, immediately my mind went to this story in the book of Job.

Elihu was the youngest of all the friends of Job. Because of his age, he waited until those who were older than him gave their thoughts to Job before he gave his. By the way, this is certainly the proper thing to do. In any situation, we should always defer to age before we decide to give an answer. However, this is not what I want you to see in this story. Elihu makes a statement in verse 7 that the *"...multitude of years should teach wisdom."* When you look at what this young man was saying, you realize that he was not giving a glowing report to those older than he. In fact, he was chastising them for their lack of wisdom in dealing with Job.

Years don't always have wisdom to teach. Age does not always mean that someone is right. Each and every one of us must be careful about thinking that someone is right just because they have some years to their life. If age is the measuring stick of right, then many heathen people who are aged and yet have no wisdom could teach us the wrong way of life. Age is never the measuring stick in determining whether or not someone is right. The Bible is the measuring stick of right and wrong.

We should always check a person's stance on a subject by the Bible. If their stance is against the Word of God, then their stance is wrong no matter what their age, position or who they are. The multitude of years should teach wisdom, but remember this is not always the case. Let us remember that sometimes the younger person could be right if the younger person's stance on a subject lines up with the Word of God. Let us be a people whose belief on a subject is determined by the Bible and not by the age of a person. Let us keep the Bible as the measurement of truth.

The Result of Seeing God

Job 42:5-6
"I have heard of thee by the hearing of the ear: but now mine eye seeth thee. Wherefore I abhor myself, and repent in dust and ashes."

One of the greatest problems I see as I travel to churches is seen in these two verses. After God responds to Job and demands of Job to give an answer, Job responds back to God by saying: because he had seen God he abhorred himself. The word *"abhor"* is a very powerful word that means "to hate extremely, or with contempt." In other words, it would mean that Job literally detested himself once he was in the presence of God. Notice, Job did not talk about how great of a Christian he was; instead he repented in dust and ashes. Once he was in the presence of God, he saw how filthy and vile he truly was.

The problem I see in churches today is people think they are really spiritual and close to God. Yet, they never walk an aisle during the invitation time and portray themselves as if they never do wrong. When I look in the Bible and see people who are close to God, I never see them talking about how good they are but I always see them realizing how terrible they are. Why is this? This is because the closer you are to God the more God's righteousness will shine a light on your unrighteousness. When a person never walks an aisle to get right with God after the preaching, they are simply telling on themselves and revealing how far away they are from God. Those people who are truly close to God will find themselves regularly at the altar repenting of their sins because God's righteousness convicts them of their unrighteousness.

Today, ask yourself how good you think you truly are. Ask yourself when you last walked an aisle. Do you find yourself worried about what others think of you? If you do, then most likely you are pretty far from God, for when a person comes into the presence of God, they will completely forget about everyone else. God's presence takes preeminence in a person's life when that person is near God.

Let each of us be one who strives for the presence of God in our lives. Let us be ready to see ourselves as we truly are when we do come into the presence of God. Once you see yourself as you truly are, I can guarantee that you will no longer think that you are someone great. Instead, you will see yourself as Job saw himself which will bring you to the point where you will *"abhor"* and detest yourself. When we reach this point in our lives, this is when God can truly do greater things through us. When we bring ourselves to the point where we are nothing and He is everything, then God can work through us as He desires. We can only acquire this attitude by being in God's presence.

A Hatred of Life

Ecclesiastes 2:17
"Therefore I hated life; because the work that is wrought under the sun is grievous unto me: for all is vanity and vexation of spirit."

What a terrible statement it is when someone says that they hate life. As Solomon is talking about his life, he simply says that he *"hated life."* Why is it that the preacher in this verse would say that he *"hated life?"* The answer can be seen in verse one of this chapter when he says, *"I said in mine heart, Go to now..."* The problem with Solomon was that he was living for the now and not for tomorrow. He was more concerned with what he had today instead of laying aside for when he would go to Heaven. This type of living is a product of selfishness.

Do you hate life right now? Have you found yourself hating the very thing that is supposed to be enjoyed? Listen, the word "life" carries the intentions of being vibrant and alive. Life is something that is to be filled with joy and happiness. God wants each of us to be able to enjoy our lives. So when a person gets to the point where they hate life, they have come to a point in their life that God did not intend for them to endure. The biggest reason for people hating life is simply that they are living for the now.

Teenager, if you hate life, it is because you are living for the now. Simply put, you are living for you. Adult, if you hate life it is because you are living for you. Married person, if you hate your married life, it is because you are living for the now in your marriage which means everything revolves around you. I could go on and on with singling out different people, but I believe you get the picture. The only reason why a person would hate life is because they live for the now which is all about them. This type of living will never satisfy and will only lead to a person hating their life.

What is the answer? The answer is to stop living for the now and start living to lay aside treasures in Heaven. In other words, start living for others and you will start seeing that life is enjoyable again. To those who hate life, what you need to do is start living your life to help everyone else. Forget about yourself and living for yourself, and you will find that your hatred for life will be turned into a love for life. In other words, make life about trying to help others enjoy life and about meeting the needs of others. Living for others is where true satisfaction comes from and this will cause a person to love life.

Today, instead of making everything about you and living for you, go out and live for others. Live for others by helping others throughout each day. Make today a day when you try to help as many people as you can. At the end of the day, you will find that life was fun and satisfying and that you loved life today. Don't be a person who hates life, become a person who loves life by helping and living for others.

Consider

Ecclesiastes 7:14
"In the day of prosperity be joyful, but in the day of adversity consider: God also hath set the one over against the other, to the end that man should find nothing after him."

I have made the statement many times, "Life is a series of mountains and valleys." If you have lived for any length of time, you no doubt understand that life has its ups and downs. At times, life will be great and then life will become hard. However, life is a series of mountains and valleys. In this verse, we are told what to do in the mountains and valleys of life.

God tells us, *"In the day of prosperity be joyful,..."* When the days come when everything is going well, you had better enjoy those days to their fullest. In other words, what God wants you to learn is that when times are good, enjoy the goodness that you have. For instance, while your health is good, use your health to its fullest and enjoy having good health. When finances are plenteous, be joyful over the fact that you have finances to take care of your needs. What God wants you to do is to stop griping over what you don't have and enjoy what you do have. Too many people in the good times complain about what they don't have and don't enjoy what God has given to them. You had better enjoy what you have because the day of adversity is going to come. When it comes, you will wish you had the day of prosperity back. So while you have the day of prosperity, enjoy it.

Then we are told to *"consider"* in the day of adversity. The word *"consider"* means "to ponder; to study; to meditate on; to view with careful examination." In other words, when adversity comes in life, instead of looking at the adversity, God wants you to consider your life. Let me give you a few things you can consider when adversity comes your way.

First of all, consider how good God has been to you. Instead of complaining about the adversity, you ought to look at life and remember how good God has been to you to give you what you have.

Second, consider that in your life you have probably had more good than bad. In most cases, God has blessed us far more than He has sent hard times our way. What happens to most when adversity comes is that the adversity seems to overtake our minds and seems to be bigger than all the good that we have had in the past. This is why you must stop and consider your whole life, and realize you have had more good in life than bad.

Third, consider that you don't have it as bad as others. Somebody somewhere has it worse than you. You ought to consider that you don't have it as bad as others do.

Fourth, consider what God is trying to teach you in times of adversity. Let me remind you that God sends adversity to help you grow and to show you things that you need to correct in your life. Take the time to consider what God wants you to correct and correct it. Consider where God wants you to grow, and be sure to grow in that area.

Last, consider that you are going to a place someday where there will be no adversity. Just remember that Heaven is not that far away. One day soon, we all will be in that place called Heaven, and all adversity will be gone forever. Let's let the day of adversity become a day of joy by considering these areas.

The Best of the Best

Song of Solomon 2:1
"I am the rose of Sharon, and the lily of the valleys."

Sharon was a city in the plains east of Jerusalem that was famous for its flowers. When God says He is the *"rose of Sharon,"* He is explaining to us what He wants to be in our lives.

When a person thinks of the most beautiful flower, I believe the majority of people would think of a rose. When a man wants to give flowers to his wife or girlfriend, probably the flower that is most known to be given is a rose. To me, the rose is the best and prettiest of all the flowers.

I believe this is what God is trying to get across to us. He is saying that He is the best of the best. He is the prettiest of the pretty. This verse is teaching us that God wants to be the best of the best in our life. It is saying that God wants to be the preeminent One in our lives.

I ask you, are you so in love with God that He is the best of the best in your life? If you had to choose between God and making money, would you choose God? If you had to choose between your house and God, would you choose God over your house? Think about this question, don't just flippantly answer it. If you had to choose between God and your most prized possession, which would you choose? God wants to be the One in your life Whom you would choose over anything else.

When I think of these statements, I am reminded of the old evangelist Charles Weigle. One night when he came home from a revival meeting, his wife met him at the table and told him he had to choose between her and God. She said, if he chose her, then he would have to stop preaching. If he chose God, she said she would leave him. Bro. Weigle looked at his wife, and with a broken heart told her that if she put it that way, he would choose God. That night his wife walked out on him because he chose God over her. Yet it was that same night, with a broken heart, that he wrote the great song, "No One Ever Cared For Me Like Jesus."

I ask you, is God the *"rose of Sharon"* in your life? Is He the best of the best to you? God wants to be the One Who consumes your heart and life. Among all the choices that we could choose in life, He wants us to choose Him over anything else. Let us throughout this day make God the *"rose of Sharon"* in our lives. Let us today and everyday make Him the best of the best.

A Formula for God's Blessings

Isaiah 2:3

"And many people shall go and say, Come ye, and let us go up to the mountain of the LORD, to the house of the God of Jacob; and he will teach us of his ways, and we will walk in his paths: for out of Zion shall go forth the law, and the word of the LORD from Jerusalem."

In this chapter, the Prophet Isaiah describes Jerusalem and Judah in the last days. He talked of the blessings of God and the desire of the people to serve God. What a wonderful sight this must have been to see revival amongst the people of God. I find in this verse a formula for the blessings of God upon the life of a nation and for that matter an individual.

First, we see there is a desire in the people. Notice the verse says, *"And many people shall go and say, Come..."* This is nothing more than a desire by the people to be around God. You will never have a personal revival in your heart without first of all desiring to have revival. I fear far too many times, when we have our revival meetings, that most people could care less if they have revival. If you want the fires of revival to burn in your soul, then you must have a desire for it.

Second, you see the people acted upon their desire. Notice again in this verse that it says, *"Come ye, and let us go up to the mountain of the LORD."* These people not only had a desire for revival, but they acted upon that desire. Let me put it very plain and simple, desire is not enough. You can have all the desire in the world for God to send revival, but you must act upon your desire. What action should we take? The very same action these people took by going to the house of the LORD. In other words, go to church! Why were these people going to church? They knew that was the place where God's Word was preached. You will never have revival personally or nationally without the Word of God. We must have a desire for revival, but we must also act upon our desire by going to church, hearing the preaching of the Word of God, and by reading the Word of God ourselves.

Third, they listened to the teaching of the Word of God. Notice this verse says, *"...and he will teach us of his ways."* Once we get to church or open the Bible to read It, we must let the Holy Spirit of God teach us His Word. This would mean you better attend a church that preaches the Word of God without reservation and you must read the Word of God with a desire to learn God's Word. I ask you, do you already have your mind made up that you know what the preacher is going to preach before he preaches? We should listen to preaching and read the Word of God with open hearts and minds to learn from God's Word what God wants to teach us.

Last of all, we see obedience. We see in this verse that the people said, *"...we will walk in his paths."* Revival comes when we act upon what we have been taught. Though it may seem hard to obey the Bible, we must walk in the paths of the Bible if we are to have revival.

Do you want revival? Then get a desire for it, act upon it by going to church and reading your Bible, listen to the Holy Spirit as He teaches you, and then obey what you have been taught. If you do this, I can guarantee you will have a revival in your heart which will result in the blessings of God on your life.

Woe Unto Them...

Isaiah 5:8

"Woe unto them that join house to house, that lay field to field, till there be no place, that they may be placed alone in the midst of the earth!"

Six times in Isaiah chapter five God pronounces a *"Woe"* upon His people. When God says to His people *"Woe,"* He is pronouncing grief, sorrow, misery and heavy calamity upon them. This is what the word *"Woe"* means. Let me show you the six areas where God pronounces this *"Woe"* upon His people so that we don't find ourselves doing the same things they did.

In verse eight God says, *"Woe unto them that join house to house."* You must understand Jewish customs to understand what God is talking about here. God never wanted His people to sell their inheritance. In other words, God tells us that when we move that which is inherited concerning who we are, there will come grief and misery upon us. Let me explain further, don't change the heritage of our fundamental methods for the methods and philosophies of liberals. We must be careful about changing who we are for the sake of getting along with others. Likewise America, we must be careful about changing our heritage of what our forefathers gave us for political correctness. Just to make it short, leave your heritage alone! Don't change it!

Second, in verse eleven, God pronounces a *"Woe"* upon those who rise early and go all day just to drink strong drink. Let me emphatically say that alcohol is still the Devil's juice. We live in a drunken society that must be stopped. I was recently talking to a police officer in a larger city who said that a survey was done in their city to see how much alcohol was involved in crime. He said that alcohol was involved in 92% of the crime in their city. I will tell you, this is true all over. NOTHING good comes from alcohol. It only brings misery and sorrow.

Third, in verse eighteen God pronounces a *"Woe"* upon those who continue to add to their own sin. In other words, God says grief and sorrow will come to those who aren't bothered by doing wrong. It should bother you when you do wrong and you should want to stop it.

Fourth, in verse twenty, God pronounces a *"Woe"* upon those who call good evil and evil good. When we have a society that has turned good into bad and bad into good, then we have a society that is headed for grief. When abortion is legal and those who say it is murder are considered weird, then evil has become good. When sodomite marriages are an accepted lifestyle, then evil is considered good.

Fifth, in verse twenty-one God pronounces a *"Woe"* upon those who are *"wise in their own eyes."* This is nothing more than pride of heart. This is talking about those who always think they're right. Let me be blunt, you are not always right. Sometimes we become legends in our own mind. Let us be careful about always trying to top everyone with how much we know and do.

Last, in verse twenty-two and twenty-three, we see God pronounce a *"Woe"* upon those who spread false reports. Let us be careful about being gossips. Let us not be guilty of spreading a false report about someone just for the sake of furthering our cause.

In each of these instances, let us be careful to make sure that we are not guilty of contributing to these *"woe"* areas. Let us not be the one guilty of causing a *"Woe"* upon our nation because we are the one who commits these horrible sins.

His Hand Is Stretched Out Still

Isaiah 9:21

"Manasseh, Ephraim; and Ephraim, Manasseh: and they together shall be against Judah. For all this his anger is not turned away, but his hand is stretched out still."

Praise God for His mercy and for His undying love! Even in the midst of His judgment, His hand is still outstretched to His people waiting and wanting them to come back to Him. In this chapter, God tells us of the wickedness of His people and what He will have to do to them. Yet, each time he ends by saying, *"...but his hand is stretched out still."* Thank God for His outstretched hand of God that is willing to take us back even though we have done something wrong.

I say to the person who feels that they have embarrassed God; His hand is stretched out still. To the one who has gone into "deep" sin and literally ruined your life; His hand is stretched out still. To the child who has gone wayward and rebelled against your parents, let me remind you that His hand is stretched out still. To the one who is addicted to the filth of pornography and the illicit lifestyle that it brings; His hand is still outstretched waiting for you to come back. To the one who is addicted to the vices of drugs and alcohol; His hand is outstretched still. To the one who is controlled by anger, gossip, backbiting, filthy language and deception; His hand is still stretched out waiting for you to come back to Him. No matter what the degree of sin you have committed, the Devil will try to trick you into believing that God would never want you back. Just like the father of the prodigal son, God is waiting for you to grab His outstretched hand so that He can help you come back to Him.

Let me take this thought one step further. If God can find in Himself to always want us back no matter what we have done, then we also should be willing to take back those who have wronged us. To the one whose spouse has been unfaithful to you, stretch out your hand and accept your spouse back. Be ready and willing to help them come back to you when they reach out to you. When a Christian has messed up their life in sin, may each of us be willing to have our hand stretched out so at the very action of them reaching out to us, we are willing to bring them back to us. Whatever the sin, whatever the infraction, we should be a people who, like our God, are ever willing with our hand outstretched to take back those who have messed up their lives.

Let us be more willing to take people back to the fold of doing right than we are to destroy them because they have gone astray. Taking people back once they have done wrong is the Christian thing to do. Let us do the right thing.

Is This the Man?

Isaiah 14:16
"They that see thee shall narrowly look upon thee, and consider thee, saying, Is this the man that made the earth to tremble, that did shake kingdoms;"

There is not a person alive who is not capable of succumbing to the temptations of the Devil. Every person, according to the Bible, is a sinner. Probably one of the greatest battles we all fight is the battle to overcome the temptation of sin. Now I do not believe that the Devil is the one who tempts us with all the temptations that we face, but I will say that all temptation of sin started with the Devil tempting us to do wrong.

As we come to the fourteenth chapter of Isaiah, God reminds us of the destination of the Devil. God told us about his beginning in Heaven; he was one of the angels of Heaven. God told us of his fall from Heaven because of his pride in trying to lift himself up above God. God also told us that the Devil will one day be bound and cast into Hell for ever and ever. God says in that day we will look at him and will be amazed that he is the one who caused all the heartache that we have seen in our life and in this world. In fact, God says that we will one day ask the question, *"Is this the man that made the earth to tremble..."*

What God is trying to get us to understand is that we have no reason to be afraid of the Devil. If we could see who he really is and how frail he truly is, then we would never give in to him. We must understand the Devil cannot do anything to God's people without first getting permission from God. So, if we are saved, we are protected by God Himself.

My question to you is this, why would you cower to the pressure that he puts on you? You must realize that his day is coming. The Devil uses people to put peer pressure on us to do wrong. Most of the wrong we do is all because we are so worried about what man is going to do to us. Let me remind you Christian, you have no reason to fear the Devil. He may attack your name through gossip, but you must remember that you have God on your side. The Devil attacks your family through the TV screen and through the pressures of society, but you must not give in to his tactics. When the Devil tries to get you to be afraid of letting others at work or at school know that you are a Christian, but don't listen to him for he cannot hurt you. Let me assure you, his day is coming.

The next time he comes and tries to tempt you to do wrong, just remember that one day you will look on him and say, *"Is this the man?"* One day we will come and see him for who he really is, and when that day comes, we do not want to have yielded to his temptations. Let us live life in such a way that we will not be ashamed of how we cowered to his threats. Let us live a life remembering that the day is coming when he will forever be bound in Hell. Take courage Christian, you are on the winning side.

A Fading Flower

Isaiah 28:1
"Woe to the crown of pride, to the drunkards of Ephraim, whose glorious beauty is a fading flower, which are on the head of the fat valleys of them that are overcome with wine!"

In this verse a warning is given to the tribe of Ephraim concerning their spirituality. When God chose to describe the spirituality of this tribe, He said that their spirituality was like a fading flower. The word *"fading"* in this verse means "to lose color; decaying; declining or withering." In other words, God was saying that Ephraim was like a dying flower. The problem with Ephraim was that they were looking to their spirituality in the past to determine how spiritual they were in the present. However, God said the problem with doing this is that they had become no more than a dying flower. If they continued to go down this path, they would eventually be completely dead.

If you have ever watched a flower as it begins to die, you notice that a flower keeps its color even though it is dying. The petals begin to fall off little by little and then eventually, if you keep the flower long enough, the petals will turn brown.

As I think of this, I think of many Christians today who rely on their past spirituality instead of looking at where they are right now. If you were to look at them through the eyes of God, I am afraid that God would see many Christians who are nothing more than a spiritually fading flower. The danger of this is that little by little they are dying and don't even see it themselves. Eventually if a Christian keeps relying upon the past to determine their spirituality instead of the present, they will die.

Let me ask you, are you a fading flower? Are you constantly talking about what you used to do in the past instead of doing something today? Did you read more Bible in the past than what you do today? Did you pray more and more fervently in the past than what you do today? Are you talking about all you used to do in the church to try to impress people with your spirituality? Did you go soul winning more in the past than you do today? The truth is, I could go on and on with each spiritual thing, but you know if you are doing more today than what you did in the past. This is even the problem with our nation; we have relied upon what God did for us in the past to call ourselves a Christian nation. The truth is, America is the farthest thing from being a Christian nation.

Let me bring this down to a more personal level. What area of your spiritual life has become a fading flower? Oh, I know that there are parts of our lives that are spiritually strong. Yet, I also know that there are parts of our spiritual lives that are starting to fade and are not where they used to be. How careful we must be that we don't let part of our spiritual lives fade away and die. We must be strong in every area of our spiritual life so that we can be what God wants us to be.

Each of us needs to constantly be careful that we don't rely upon our past service to God to determine whether or not we are right with God today. Every day we need to do what it takes to be right with God. Every day we need to pray, read our Bible and obey what God has commanded us to do. Be careful that you do not become a fading flower.

Their Day Is Coming

Isaiah 37:37-38
"So Sennacherib king of Assyria departed, and went and returned, and dwelt at Nineveh. And it came to pass, as he was worshipping in the house of Nisroch his god, that Adrammelech and Sharezer his sons smote him with the sword; and they escaped into the land of Armenia: and Esarhaddon his son reigned in his stead."

Judah had just gone through the great revival that came in Hezekiah's day and you would think that everything would go their way. However, when God blesses, the Devil always fights. This is the case in this story with the nation of Judah.

Sennacherib, King of Assyria, came and threatened Judah that he was going to take them away into another land. He told them not to listen to Hezekiah because he could not save them from his hand. He reminded Judah of what he had done to every other country and told them he would do the same to them. I can only imagine the fear that came upon the hearts of the people of Judah. However, they did the right thing by calling upon God and asking Him to help them, and He did help them. We read in this verse that God sent another country against Assyria that killed many of their troops. The Bible states that when Sennacherib went back to his own country, his own sons killed him with the sword. What a shameful way to die! However, this is a reminder to every Christian that the day of the heathen will soon end, and their day of shame and sorrow will come.

I want to encourage and remind every Christian who reads this, that the day of the heathen will soon end. Yes, it seems this old world is getting worse and worse. It seems as if the heathen are getting away with their wicked lifestyle. It seems as if living right does not pay. However, just remember, their day is coming.

I say to the Christian teenager who tries to do right in the public school but has become the joke of the whole school, their day is coming. To the person who works in the factory or office place and tries to live right amongst a bunch of people who mock your Christian life, just remember that their day is coming. To the Christian who sees Hollywood, liberal politicians and heathen people do everything they can to destroy our way of living and who make a mockery of serving God, may I remind you that their day will come.

So, take courage and keep living right remembering their day is coming. Don't you dare give in to their threats and jokes, but instead keep on doing right remembering their day will come. My whole purpose in writing this is to encourage those who are just about ready to give in to the threats of the heathen. Let me remind you their day will come and your stand for doing right will be vindicated.

God's Counseling Session

Isaiah 25:1
"O LORD, thou art my God; I will exalt thee, I will praise thy name; for thou hast done wonderful things; thy counsels of old are faithfulness and truth."

Have you ever wondered what God would say to you if you went into His office and asked counsel about what you should do with your life? Have you ever had a time when you just wanted to ask God what you should do with your life? Well, I believe we have in this verse the answer that God would give you if you were to ask His advice. This verse says, *"...thy counsels of old are faithfulness and truth."*

Yes, this is what God would counsel you if you sat in His office and He gave you counsel on what to do in life. God would first of all tell you to be faithful in life. In other words, in every thing you do for God, you should be faithful. We should be faithful in our marriages. Every spouse reading this devotional needs to realize that God would have you to be faithful to your vows and to your spouse. We should also be faithful to our church and the duties that we are responsible for at our church. Just be faithful! Be faithful to the Word of God. Be faithful to the calling of God upon your life. Be faithful to the truths of the Word of God. Be faithful to the fundamentals of the faith. Whatever you do, follow God's advice and be faithful.

You say to me, Bro. Domelle, how can I be faithful? I will answer this question by telling you a story of a lady who has taught her Sunday school class for over 75 years. One day she came to her pastor and said to him, "Pastor, do you know how I have been faithful to my Sunday school class all these years?" The pastor told me he was expecting some great piece of wisdom to come from her lips. Her explanation to her pastor of how she was faithful all those years was this, she said, "For 75 years I just showed up." That is what it takes to be faithful. You must do what you are supposed to do when you feel like it and when you don't feel like it. The way to be faithful is to just show up and fulfill your responsibilities whatever they may be.

Secondly, if God was to counsel us some more, He would tell us to do right. Not only does God want us to be faithful, He also wants us to do right while we are being faithful. As Dr. Bob Jones Sr. used to say, "Do right even if the stars fall." Anybody can do right because doing right is always a choice. So when God counsels us in life about what we ought to do, His counsel is to do right. Do right when others aren't doing right. Do right when the leaders of the church are not doing right. Do right when your parents don't do right. Do right when your friends stop doing right. Do right when your heroes stop doing right. If the whole world stops doing right, do right!

In these two pieces of advice from God, we find that everything in life will take care of itself if we will just be faithful and do right. Become the type of person who decides that no matter what may come your way in life, you are going to be faithful and do right no matter what the consequence of doing right may be.

Your Central Processing Unit

Proverbs 4:23
"Keep thy heart with all diligence; for out of it are the issues of life."

Everything in life comes from the heart. I like to say that the heart is the central processing unit of life. According to this verse, every issue of life comes from the heart.

The heart is the seat of your affections. The heart is where your passions of life come from. The heart is the place where your love comes from. The heart is the place from where you receive joy. The heart is the place where your will is determined. The heart is the place where your purposes of life and designs of life are formed. The heart is the very center of your life from which good or bad comes.

Because your heart is the center from which everything you do in life comes, you must be careful what you feed your heart. Your heart will process those things which you feed it. Just like a computer processes the information that is fed into it, likewise the heart processes what you put into it as well. If you put trash into your heart, you can only expect trash to come out. If you put good into your heart, you can expect good to come out. Whatever you feed your heart is eventually what will come out of it, and it will eventually determine what you will do. This is why God said to keep your *"heart with all diligence."* The word *"keep"* means "to guard." God warns us and even commands us to guard what we let into our heart, for whatever we let in, we will become.

How do I guard my heart? You guard your heart by guarding what you read, what you hear, what you watch and with whom you choose to spend time. These are the areas from which your heart gets its information. If you watch the wrong things, then the heart will process the wrong things out. In whatever area of life you are having problems; you are having problems in that area because you are feeding your heart bad things in that area.

I ask you, what are you feeding your heart? What have you watched lately? What have you been looking at and reading lately? Who have you been spending time with lately? What have you been listening to lately? Whatever you feed your heart, you will eventually do. So you must ask yourself this question, "Do I want to become what I am feeding my heart?" If you don't, then stop feeding it! This week, be extra careful about what you feed your heart. Let's guard it realizing that we will become whatever we feed or put into our heart.

A Portion with the Great

Isaiah 53:12
"Therefore will I divide him a portion with the great, and he shall divide the spoil with the strong; because he hath poured out his soul unto death: and he was numbered with the transgressors; and he bare the sin of many, and made intercession for the transgressors."

In chapter fifty-three Isaiah prophetically tells us of the coming Messiah. In this chapter he gave hope to the people of Israel that the Messiah would come and die for the sins of mankind. Isaiah told us what the Messiah would have to go through when He came. As we see the suffering that the Messiah would have to go through, we come to the last verse of this chapter and see a statement that God makes about the Messiah that could truly help us understand how to become great among men. God said that because the Messiah *"poured out his soul unto death:"* that God would *"divide him a portion with the great."* In other words, though the Messiah was not looking for greatness and simply poured out his soul even unto the point that He would die for us, this action caused Him to be great among men.

This is exactly how a person becomes a great person. In our society many people, both in the spiritual realm as well as in the worldly realm, are so worried about their legacies. Because they are worried about their legacies, they promote themselves and try to get people to look at them and praise them. This is not how a person becomes great. If a person is to become great, they must lose themselves in the cause of doing right, even to the point that they are willing to die for that cause. This is the action that will cause them to become great. You check every great person in history and you will find that they became a great person, not by seeking to become great, but by pouring out their soul in what they did.

Though you may not be interested in becoming a great individual or having a great legacy that lives on for years after you are gone, you can still learn from great people. Learn to pour your soul into everything that you do. Parent, if you want to become great in the eyes of your child, then pour your life into helping your children turn out right. Stop worrying about what they think of you at the present time and simply pour your soul into parenting. Likewise, the same can be said about a school teacher, or a Sunday school teacher, or anyone who may lead in any area. Don't be concerned with what people think of you at the present. Pour your soul into helping those you lead, and you will find, in the future, you will be a great person in the minds of those whom you poured your soul into. This world needs people who are not worried about their legacy, but who are concerned with pouring themselves into everything they do.

Be careful that you don't become a half-hearted individual. Whenever you do something no matter what it may be, pour your soul and lose yourself into that activity. By doing so, you will find yourself one day being mentioned among the great people of history by those in whom you invested. Stop looking for greatness, just serve people and causes like greatness does; by pouring your whole soul into everything that you do.

Two Requirements for God's Blessings

Isaiah 56:2

"Blessed is the man that doeth this, and the son of man that layeth hold on it; that keepeth the sabbath from polluting it, and keepeth his hand from doing any evil."

To be blessed by God, I would imagine, is the desire of every person. A person knows that if they are blessed of God then certainly life will be a joy to live. However, what does it mean to be blessed and how can we get blessed by God?

The word *"blessed"* means "to be happy." In other words, when God says, *"Blessed is the man,"* God is saying, "Happy is the man." The man who does what God tells us to do in this verse will be a happy person who is in favor with God. How can you become a blessed man? God says, in this verse, there are two ways you can be blessed.

First of all, God says the person that *"keepeth the sabbath from polluting it,..."* The Sabbath was a very important day for the Jew. It was a day that was to be set aside for the LORD as this was His day. God did not want any work to be done on this day. God wanted His people to spend this day thinking of Him. Today, the Sabbath has been replaced with Sunday. We do not observe the ordinances of the Sabbath because they were done away with at Calvary. However, we do celebrate the resurrection of Jesus every Sunday. We call this the LORD's Day. I am still the old-fashioned type of person who believes God will bless those who keep Sunday as a day to go to church. Our society has taken Sundays and polluted our Sundays with entertainment. If we want God to bless us, then I believe we should still make Sundays a day to go to church. Don't be the type of person who looks for reasons to stay out of church. Look for reasons to be in church.

Secondly, God says He will bless the person who keeps their *"hand from doing any evil."* In other words, God's blessings are upon the person who does everything they can to try not to hurt people. I know you think that there are not many people like this, but the truth is many of us do things that hurt people every day. For instance, when you try to get revenge with someone, you are trying to do evil to someone. Let me even get a little more personal. When you try to cut someone off on the road that cut you off, you are doing evil. When a spouse throws something up from the past in an argument, they are being evil. When brothers and sisters tattle on each other to get them into trouble, they are trying to hurt each other. When people gossip about someone, they are trying to hurt an individual. Evil is doing anything that would hurt someone. Avoid anything that would be evil or hurtful to someone if you want God to bless you.

In this verse, we find a simple formula for how we can receive the blessings of God. To put it simply, to be blessed of God we should make sure that we have a right relationship with God and also have a right relationship with man. When you do this, your life will be blessed.

The Bigness of God

Isaiah 66:1
"Thus saith the LORD, The heaven is my throne, and the earth is my footstool: where is the house that ye build unto me? and where is the place of my rest?"

When you were a child, do you remember how big your dad seemed to you? When I was a child I use to think that my dad was a big man. I would look at his muscles and think about how strong my dad was, and I would think, "My, look how strong dad is." Yet now I look at my dad and truthfully, my dad has never been a big man. However, in the eyes of a little boy, no one was bigger than dad. Because I thought my dad was so big, I was never afraid or worried around him. I felt that my dad was big enough to handle anything.

Christian, let me remind you how big your God is today. The Bible says that the heavens are His throne and the Earth is His footstool. Just to give you a few facts to show you how big God is, the Earth alone is 24,902.4 miles in circumference. The surface area of the Earth is 196,950,000 miles. What a big Earth! Yet, the Bible states that the Earth is his footstool. We cannot even measure the heavens for they are infinite in size. Yet, the Bible states that the heavens are His throne.

As you think about this, don't you think that God is big enough to handle your problems? I would imagine that the problems you are having today are not too big for God. Christian, you have a big God Who can certainly handle all of your problems.

Are you having problems in a relationship? Let me remind you that God is big enough to handle your problems. Are you having financial struggles? Just remember that God is big enough to handle your problems. Are you struggling with your health today? Let me remind you that you serve a big God Who is capable of handling all of your problems. Do you struggle in school and wonder if God can help you with your studies? I promise you, your problems with your studies are not too big for God. No matter what your problem is today, God is a big God Who is capable of handling ALL of your problems.

I know this life throws many problems at us, but we must keep our eyes on the bigness of God. Let me assure you that even though our problems may overwhelm us, they do not overwhelm God. He is big enough and strong enough to handle any problem that you may face today.

Because of this, you need not fear and you need not be afraid in life, for whatever life throws at you today and in the future, GOD CAN HANDLE YOUR PROBLEMS! Christian, whatever the problem you are facing today, run to Him and ask Him for His help. He is more than willing to help you because you belong to Him. You don't need to be afraid, and you don't need to fear the problem. If you will keep your eyes on the bigness of God, you will realize there is nothing that He cannot handle.

The Symbol Is Not Greater Than the Object

Jeremiah 3:16
"And it shall come to pass, when ye be multiplied and increased in the land, in those days, saith the LORD, they shall say no more, The ark of the covenant of the LORD: neither shall it come to mind: neither shall they remember it; neither shall they visit it; neither shall that be done any more."

Though this verse is talking about the last days when Christ will rule upon the Earth, I believe there is a truth we can learn. Notice the phrase, *"...The ark of the covenant of the LORD: neither shall it come to mind: neither shall they remember it..."* The truth that God was teaching His people is very evident. It seemed as if these people were more tied to the Ark of the Covenant than they were to God. The Ark of the Covenant was only a symbol of the presence of God and was there to point God's people to Him. Instead the symbol became the object they cherished more than the One Who gave them the object.

How careful we must be that we as Christians don't think we are spiritual because we go to church or serve in the church. One of the sins I have seen in churches is when people think their service in the church allows them to do other things that are against God. Let me be blunt with you, just because you preach a sermon, work a bus route, or even go soul winning, does not give you a license to do wrong.

We think at times that if our good outweighs our bad then God is fine with our sin. This is ludicrous and absurd! We are never justified in doing wrong, and God does not justify our sin no matter what we do for Him. If God will judge Moses for his disobedience, then I am sure He will judge us for our sin no matter what we do for Him.

Let's be careful that we don't think our spiritual actions give us a pass to sin. Let us always remember that God expects us to do right all the time. Don't be guilty of passing off your sin because you are busy in the church. Get rid of sin and do right realizing this is the desire that God has for all of His people.

Results of Complaining

Jeremiah 8:10
"Therefore will I give their wives unto others, and their fields to them that shall inherit them: for every one from the least even unto the greatest is given to covetousness, from the prophet even unto the priest every one dealeth falsely."

Maybe one of the saddest things I have seen in my life is when a person works hard for something their whole life and then because of sin someone else enjoys the fruits of their labors. When this happens, it a travesty!

This is what God was showing us in this verse concerning the wise men of that day. Because they thought they knew better than God and rejected God's Word to live their own lifestyle, God said the day would come when other men would enjoy their wives, and their enemies would inherit their lands. All of this would happen because they rejected God's Word.

Notice the sin that God pointed out which led to this judgment was the sin of covetousness. What a wicked sin covetousness is! Here God had given them plenty, yet they felt it was not enough. They were a people who always wanted more. They were a people who always wanted what everybody else had and were never satisfied with what they had. They always thought that what they had was not enough even though they had been blessed in a great way.

Maybe the greatest sin of Christianity and of our society today is the sin of covetousness. It is amazing to me how people constantly complain about what they do not have and how God has not been good to them. Let me suggest you go and look in your closet and see how many clothes and shoes you have. Let me suggest you go and look in your cupboards and see how much food you have. Let me suggest you look at the house you live in and see how nice and big it is. Let me suggest you look in your garage or driveway and count how many cars you have. We complain constantly that our house is not nice enough. Let me ask you, how nice does it have to be before you stop complaining? We complain constantly about not having enough money. Again, let me ask you how much money is enough money before you stop complaining about how much money you don't have? The truth is if you did get what you said you wanted, you still would not be happy because your pattern is once you get something, you complain again that it is not nice enough.

You better be careful about the sin of covetousness because if God judges you like He did these people, He will take away from you what you do have and others will enjoy what you would not enjoy. My advice is to be content with what you have, and thank God for the blessings He has sent your way.

Be very careful about complaining about what you do not have and be a person who is happy with what you do have. When you are happy with what you have, when God gives you more, it will be a bonus to you. Let us be content and not covetous.

Take Heed to Yourselves

Jeremiah 17:21
"Thus saith the LORD; Take heed to yourselves, and bear no burden on the sabbath day, nor bring it in by the gates of Jerusalem;"

As God tried to warn the kings of Judah and the people of Judah of His anger against them for their sins, He warned them in this verse to *"...Take heed to yourselves...* concerning the Sabbath day. God was warning them to watch and be careful about observing the Sabbath day of which they were to observe. I want you to notice the phrase, *"...Take heed to yourselves..."* Let's discuss this phrase for a bit.

Seven times in the Bible God says this exact phrase. Now I know it is probably mentioned in a different way several other times, but seven times, the number of completion, God warns His people to *"...Take heed to yourselves..."* The word *"heed"* means "to mind; to regard with care; to take notice of; to attend to; to observe." In other words, God was telling the people to watch themselves with extra care and be careful. Let me talk to you about some areas in which you need to *"...Take heed to yourselves..."*

First, *"...Take heed to yourselves..."* with the opposite gender. In today's world of man and woman working so close together, we must be very careful and watch ourselves with each other. Watch yourself as you talk that you don't get loose in your conversations. I especially think that you should be very careful about texting each other on your cell phones. You may be innocent in your intentions, but the other person may take it differently. I think it best that the opposite genders don't text each other. Just be careful that you keep the proper distance with each other.

Second, *"...Take heed to yourselves..."* in the area of your marriage. Married couples, watch that you don't let anything come between you and your spouse. Keep your relationship with each other very close and don't keep secrets from each other. When your spouse comes in as you are typing emails or talking on the phone, don't hide from them what you are typing or all of a sudden change your tone to a quieter tone so they can't hear you. Be careful to keep your relationship with each other close and open.

Third, *"...Take heed to yourselves..."* when it comes to other people. All of us need to be careful to watch our tongue and what we say to others. We all must be sure to keep a good relationship with others. Listen, we must live with each other on this Earth, so let's work at keeping our relationships with each other right. Watch how you say things. Many times you can say things in a sharp tone and not realize it yourself. When you are talking to others, listen and watch how you respond to others. Don't get short with others but rather work hard at keeping a good relationship.

Last of all, *"...Take heed to yourselves..."* when it comes to your relationship with God. Be careful that you keep a good relationship with God. Watch carefully that your walk with God doesn't become cold and indifferent. Be careful that you don't become apathetic towards your walk with God. We must keep our walk with God right, for if our walk with God is not right, then every other area I mentioned cannot and will not be right.

Take inventory of all these areas today and be sure to *"...Take heed to yourselves..."* in each of these areas. If these are not right, be sure to make them right today.

Don't Have Your Hand Out

Jeremiah 22:13
"Woe unto him that buildeth his house by unrighteousness, and his chambers by wrong; that useth his neighbour's service without wages, and giveth him not for his work;"

As Jeremiah continues to pronounce God's judgment against the house of Judah, we come to this verse where God pronounced a warning to those who build something the wrong way. One of the ways that God said a person should not build something is to build it without paying for it. Notice God says, *"...that useth his neighbor's service without wages, and giveth him not for his work."* God did not like it that His people expected others to build something for them without paying them back.

I have been around Christianity my whole life. One of the things I have noticed about Christians, and I hate to say this, is that most Christians expect something for nothing. In other words, most Christians walk around with their hand out expecting everyone else to pay their way. Christians need to get away from the idea that everybody should be willing to do things for them for free. The truth is, Christians should be willing to pay their own way. Let me be honest with you, Christian businessmen have to pay their bills just like you do and it is wrong for us to use them to build our ministries and fill our coffers without paying them back. Let me give you two thoughts on this.

First, be sure to recompense people when they do something for you. When you ask someone to do something, don't expect them to do it for free. I know you may not have a lot of money, but you do need to learn to, at the least, offer to pay. If they take your money, don't be upset about it.

As many of you know I sell books and CD albums of my preaching. It is amazing to me how many people are almost offended that I won't give them these things. They come to my table or call me up telling me they don't have much money but would love to have some of my preaching albums or one of my books. Let me ask you this question, would you go into a restaurant and sit down and tell the waitress that you don't have any money but would love to have some of the food off the menu? Of course you wouldn't! So why do we do this with fellow Christians? Listen, be more willing to pay people for something than to have your hand out. You may not be able to pay a lot, but give people something out of pure appreciation.

Secondly, pay people for their work with appreciation. One of the greatest problems I see in our churches is a lack of appreciation for the work accomplished. When someone does something for you, especially if they do it for free, thank them for the work which they have done. Don't be an ungrateful person with your hand out expecting everyone to give you something. Christians need to learn to say, "Thank you" all the time.

Now I am not teaching that we should not be a giving people who give of our services to the church or to others for free. What I am saying is Christians need to be careful about always walking around with their hand out and building our ministries and filling our coffers off the hard-earned wages of others. Let each of us be more willing to pay our way than to expect others to pay our way. The person who pays their own way will enjoy life more and will certainly feel much better about themselves.

Finding God in Your Life

Jeremiah 29:13
"And ye shall seek me, and find me, when ye shall search for me with all your heart."

Notice the result of getting right with God. God says when we decide to get right with Him and start seeking Him, He will always be found. The truth is God is always a God Who can be found. It is just a matter of us seeking after Him. This seeking after God is not so much to find Him as it is about us having a heart that wants Him. When God sees our heart and sees in our heart a desire for Him, then God will certainly allow us to find Him in our lives. Does this mean that God is not in our lives? Most certainly not! God wants to see our desire for Him before He reveals Himself to us.

God wants to be wanted just like you and I want to be wanted. You know what I am talking about. Have you ever been to a place where you did not feel wanted? Normally when that situation arises we find ourselves quietly slipping out because we just feel out of place. This is what God does with us. When we make Him feel that He is not wanted, He quietly slips into the background of our lives waiting for the day when we want Him again. When we show Him that we want Him, He is always found because He is right where we left Him.

I ask you, have you made God feel as though He is not wanted in your life? Could you have made God feel uncomfortable around you because you are more interested in the material things of life than you are in Him? Could you have made God feel uncomfortable around you because of the life of sin you are living? Could you have made God feel uncomfortable around you because you are more interested in worldly activities than you are in Him?

Let me warn you, you had better make God number one in your life or you will find that He will not be found in your life.

Let me also remind you, if you will seek Him with all your heart, He will reveal Himself to you again. It is up to us!

Make God feel comfortable around you every day. Talk to Him all throughout the day! Live a right life and avoid sin all throughout the day! Read His Word daily so that He feels that He has a part in your life! Whatever you do, include God in on it. By doing this you will make God feel wanted in your life and then you will notice that you will be able to find Him when you need Him which is every hour of every day.

Living a Life of Simplicity

Jeremiah 35:5-6

"But they said, We will drink no wine: for Jonadab the son of Rechab our father commanded us, saying, Ye shall drink no wine, neither ye, nor your sons for ever: Neither shall ye build house, nor sow seed, nor plant vineyard, nor have any: but all your days ye shall dwell in tents; that ye may live many days in the land where ye be strangers."

We have a story here of the house of the Rechabites who, the Bible says, would not drink wine nor would they build themselves houses in which to live. God used these people as a sermon illustration for the Prophet Jeremiah to show their obedience to their forefathers.

Jonadab, who was one of the forefathers of the Rechabites, commanded them not to drink any wine nor to build any houses in which to live. Up to this point in their history they had obeyed this command. Now I could go into a threefold purpose of why he commanded this, but I want to point out a truth that I believe we can learn from these verses. I believe one of the reasons why this father taught his children not to do this is because he wanted his children to learn to live in simplicity instead of living a life of lavishness. This father realized that the more lavish your lifestyle is the more chance you have of ruining your life.

Maybe one of the greatest mistakes I have seen in America and among Christians is the desire to live lavish lifestyles. We live such lifestyles to impress people with what we have and to show people that we are "successful." Yet the truth is, nowhere can you find that living a lavish lifestyle is a sign of success. The only reason we live such lifestyles is to impress and to show off. May I say to everyone who reads this, be careful about living a lavish lifestyle.

Be careful about always having to have the latest electronic gadgets. Be careful about always having to have new clothes.

Be careful about going into huge debt to buy huge homes to impress everyone with your "success." The clothes you wear and the cars you drive and the home you live in does not show who you truly are. The true you is what is on the inside and people are more impressed with a real person than they are with someone who tries to show everyone how "successful" they are by living a lavish lifestyle. Now don't get me wrong, I do not believe that you should not enjoy the benefits of life that God has given to you. What I believe is you should be careful about trying to live a lavish lifestyle just to impress people. Young couples should be especially careful about living lavishly while they are young. Wait until you are older to enjoy some of the benefits of your hard work.

There is nothing wrong with living simple lives. You will find that those who live simple lives rarely have complex problems when they are older. The simpler the life, the less complexity and headaches you will have. The more lavish the lifestyle, the more complex and difficult it is to keep up with that life. Enjoy life, but be careful about living life too lavishly or extravagantly. Learn to live a simple life and you will find you will have fewer headaches which will result in you enjoying your life a whole lot more.

Stop Lying to Yourself

Jeremiah 37:9
"Thus saith the LORD; Deceive not yourselves, saying, The Chaldeans shall surely depart from us: for they shall not depart."

The situation in this chapter was a very stressful situation for the people of Judah. Zedekiah had just become king; the Egyptian army had come to take over the country which caused the Chaldeans to leave the city of Jerusalem because of their fear of the impending war. Zedekiah called for Jeremiah and asked him what the future held for the war with the Egyptian army. However, as Jeremiah was asking God what was going to happen with the Egyptians, God told Jeremiah the people of Judah needed to understand that it was not the Egyptians they needed to fear, for this army would go back to Egypt. It was the Chaldeans who would come back and eventually take them into bondage. Then God made the statement that we read in the verse above, *"Deceive not yourselves..."* The reason God made this statement is because the false prophets were preaching a message of peace when captivity, because of sin, should have been preached. God was telling the people to not mislead themselves into thinking they were going to get away with their sin.

As I think of this phrase, I think about many people who deceive themselves all the time and tell themselves something that is not true. For instance, be careful about deceiving yourself about your spiritual state. Too many times we lie to ourselves about how spiritual we really are when the truth is we are backslidden and not right with God. We love to believe our own lies about our relationship with God. Listen, you are only hurting yourself when you deceive yourself about whether or not you are right with God.

Also, be careful about deceiving yourself about your health. I know this is not mentioned in this verse, but I have heard too many reports lately of people who are facing health problems.

Thankfully in each of these cases they didn't deceive themselves into saying they are fine physically. However, in many cases I hear of people who never listen to their body when it is crying out for them to get to a doctor to care for things. Don't lie to yourself, this never helps you.

Let me ask you, are you deceiving yourself about your marriage? Are you deceiving yourself about your finances? Are you deceiving yourself about your weight? Are you deceiving yourself about your walk with God? Are you deceiving yourself about how healthy you are? Are you deceiving yourself about any area of your life? The main person you are hurting when you lie to yourself is you. Not only do you hurt yourself, you also hurt those around you. Be careful about deceiving yourself, instead be a person who listens to and acknowledges the truth about yourself.

Ye Have Seen

Jeremiah 44:2

"Thus saith the LORD of hosts, the God of Israel; Ye have seen all the evil that I have brought upon Jerusalem, and upon all the cities of Judah; and, behold, this day they are a desolation, and no man dwelleth therein,"

One of the greatest teachers in life is on the job training. With all the schooling I have gone through, I have learned the most by watching what others have done. I do it if it worked for them and don't do it if it did not work for them.

I recall years ago I went fishing up in Canada with a preacher who claimed to be an expert Walleye fisherman. He took me out on the boat and told me what he did and then I watched. I saw how he started pulling up fish and I decided that this is what I wanted to do as well. It was amazing; as long as I did what he did I caught fish. However, there was another man in the boat with us who did not copy what this pastor was doing and he only caught one fish the whole morning. The only reason I was able to catch fish was because I saw what the expert fisherman did and I learned from him.

This is what God was trying to teach His people in this verse. He said, *"Ye have seen..."* all that has happened to those in Jerusalem and should have learned from them what not to do. God told the Jews in Egypt not to make the same mistake they had watched others make. You see, God was trying to teach them to learn from the mistakes of others so they wouldn't have to go through the same heartache that those who messed up had gone through.

Over and over again I watch people, one right after another, make the same mistake they watched others make and wonder why they did not learn from those who they watched mess up their lives. I watch children go down the same path of destruction that their parents took and wonder why they did not learn a lesson from their parents. Listen, one of the greatest teachers we have is those who have gone before us. We have seen what has worked and what has not worked, and we should learn from them what to and what not to do.

Be careful not to be so unobservant that you don't learn life's lessons from those who have gone before you. Don't be so hard headed that you end up going down the same path that others have taken which led to their demise. We all have seen others either succeed or fail. Take the lessons you have learned from them and apply them to your life so you can succeed and not fail. God did not allow you to see the mistakes of others for no reason. Because you have seen their mistakes, if you make the same mistakes, it is no one's fault but your own.

Be observant in life and study people so that you can learn from them and not have to go through the same hard lessons that they went through. If you take their lessons and apply them to your life, you will find life will become much simpler. Always remember to learn from the lessons of others!

Pleasant Words

Proverbs 16:24
"Pleasant words are as an honeycomb, sweet to the soul, and health to the bones."

I am sure that you have heard the phrase, "Sticks and stones may break my bones, but words will never harm me." Now this may sound good as a defense when you are a child and someone is calling you names, but the truth is this statement is a lie. I have always said that bones can heal, but unpleasant words spoken pierce the heart and many times it takes years to heal. How careful we must be with the words that we speak.

In this verse God said that *"pleasant words"* are helpful in two ways; in sweetening up a person's life and giving health to your bones. If pleasant words can make people sweeter and also give health to a person's life, then we should learn what pleasant words are and learn to speak them. The word *"pleasant"* in this verse means "to be cheerful; enlivening; happy; humorous; adapted to mirth." In other words, God wants His people to learn to be a people who speak cheerfully and happily and even humorously. The truth is many people need to learn how to lighten up a bit in life. Many people need to learn to be happy and to make people happy. What God was teaching us is that we should strive to make people sweeter and enjoy life more by the way we speak.

Recently I was preaching at a church where the pastor pointed out to me that a certain person with whom it was hard to get along. I endeavored on that trip to make that person smile and try to make that person a person with whom we could get along. Every day when I was around this person, I joked a bit and talked happily and cheerfully. Before my trip was over I had won that person over through my pleasant words.

Each of us needs to be careful to speak pleasant words all the time. We should especially strive to speak pleasant words. Our homes should not be a place of fighting and arguing. Instead, they should be a place of pleasant words which sweeten up the atmosphere of our home and give health to the relationships. Likewise, at the workplace and even in our churches we should learn to speak pleasant words.

Try to make yourself a person who sweetens up the atmosphere with your pleasant words. Everywhere you go try to be a person who makes relationships healthier and better because of the words you speak. Be careful of what you say at all the times realizing that the words which you speak influence the atmosphere of a place and also influence the health of every relationship.

Entering His Gates

Psalm 100:4
"Enter into his gates with thanksgiving, and into his courts with praise: be thankful unto him, and bless his name."

When you study the entrance into the Temple in the Old Testament, God told the High Priests that they were not to enter into His presence in just any manner. I will not cover how they were to enter, but God had prescribed a way for them to come into His presence.

Now that the vail of the Temple has been torn, God wants us to come into His presence personally. What a privilege you and I have to be able to personally come into the presence of God. This Psalm tells us, that when we come to the gates of His presence in prayer, that we are to come with thanksgiving. In other words, God said the greatest way to get God's presence in your life is to be a person who gives thanks to God all the time.

Oh how much we have to be thankful for today! Just think, you have clothes to wear, shoes on your feet, a Bible to read, a church to attend, freedom to serve the LORD, Jesus as our Saviour, the Holy Spirit as our Comforter, God as our Father, and so much more that we could not even begin to mention it all. We are certainly a people who have a lot for which to be thankful.

No matter how bad your life may seem, you have a reason to be thankful. Now God says before you ever enter into the gates of prayer, you should always come to Him with thanksgiving for what He has done for you. Always remember to give God thanks every day when you come into His presence. This not only prepares your heart for God, but it also prepares God for you.

I ask you, when is the last time you sat down to give God thanks when you went into His presence? Do you just barge into His presence without ever thanking Him for all that He has done for you? Don't be a person who is ungrateful to God for His goodness and blessings towards you. Be sure that you preface every prayer with thanksgiving.

Stand Upon Thy Feet

Ezekiel 2:1

"And he said unto me, Son of man, stand upon thy feet, and I will speak unto thee."

As Ezekiel finished describing the vision that he saw, the next thing we read is God speaking to him in this verse. God told Ezekiel to stand upon his feet, for when Ezekiel would stand up then God would speak to Him. This is interesting to me that God was not willing to speak to Ezekiel while he was sitting down, only when he was standing would God speak to him.

In my travels throughout the years, I have counseled many people who ask me how they can know what God wants them to do. My response to them is to ask them what they are doing in their church for God. You see, my experience has always been that God speaks to me while I am doing something for Him. Rarely am I sitting doing nothing when God tells me to do something. Now why is this? God chooses to speak to those who are already doing something for Him, and He tells them what to do in their life because they are already busy doing something for God. God spoke to Moses as he was walking through the wilderness. God anointed David as he was busy caring for his father's sheep. God chose Saul as he was hunting down his father's donkeys. God chooses to use people who are busy doing something.

So you want God to use you and speak to you? Then what you need to do is get busy in your church serving God, and God will use you. Get busy helping others, and God will speak to you and use you. Get busy telling others about Jesus, and God will use you. Always remember that God uses those who are busy and not those who are sitting doing nothing. So when God says, *"...stand upon thy feet..."*, what God is wanting you to do is to get busy, for when He sees you already serving Him, then He knows He can trust you when He speaks to you.

I ask you, are you standing upon your feet serving God or are you sitting waiting for God to speak to you? Stand up and get busy serving God and you will find God's hand will come upon you to use you in a way you never imagined that He could.

A Remnant

Ezekiel 14:22
"Yet, behold, therein shall be left a remnant that shall be brought forth, both sons and daughters: behold, they shall come forth unto you, and ye shall see their way and their doings: and ye shall be comforted concerning the evil that I have brought upon Jerusalem, even concerning all that I have brought upon it."

God has always used the remnant to do His major works. As you read through the Bible you will find that it was the remnant that God has chosen to do the greatest works that we talk about today. Noah was the remnant of his society. David was the remnant in the battle with Goliath. Gideon was a remnant who stood when the crowd was fleeing. Joseph was the remnant that did right when his brothers would not do right. On and on the stories of the Bible are filled with a remnant of people who decided to do right in spite of what the crowd did.

God told Ezekiel, when the judgment was over that He was going to bring upon His people, Ezekiel would find a remnant that still stood and did right. In fact, God said this remnant would be a comfort to the Prophet Ezekiel. Oh, how our nation needs a remnant today that will stand in the face of the wickedness in our society. Oh, how Christianity needs a remnant that will stand when it seems as though Christianity compromises and falls away from what is right. However, what does it take to be a remnant?

First, it takes a person who is willing to stand alone. You always notice that the remnant never runs with the crowd, they always stand alone. You will notice the remnant never sees which way the winds of the populace are blowing to decide what they are going to do. The remnant always stands alone. They stand alone on the job, in the schoolhouse, in the home, in their society and even among their own Christian movement. Yes, the remnant does not need the following of people to make their stand for they can stand alone.

Secondly, the remnant does right when others do wrong. You will always find that the remnant does right because right is the right thing to do. I look at our fundamental leaders of today and I wonder why they are not willing to be the remnant. Men who once stood for something have now changed what they once stood for because it is not popular anymore. Let me say this emphatically, right is right to do all the time! It does not matter that times have changed and others before us who stood for right are gone. Right never changes and never will change. The remnant always does right in spite of what everyone around them does.

Lastly, you will find the remnant is willing to stand up against the odds. Usually the remnant does not walk with the flow. They normally go against the flow. The remnant usually does not walk with the winds of change, but normally walks against the winds of change. The remnant does what they are supposed to do without fear of failure. The remnant would rather do right and fail than do wrong and succeed.

I ask you, are you willing to be the remnant? Oh, how we need you to stand in your place for right even when it gets hard, for it is always a remnant that saves a nation and saves a movement from falling. Decide today that for the rest of your life you will be a part of that remnant who will stand in the day of need. Today is that day of need!

Doth He Not Speak Parables?

Ezekiel 20:49
"Then said I, Ah Lord GOD! they say of me, Doth he not speak parables?"

After the Prophet Ezekiel had prophesied to the people, you see him getting frustrated when he makes the statement about what the people say of him, *"Doth he not speak parables?"* Ezekiel was getting to the point where he felt that his preaching was falling upon deaf ears. He felt that the people thought he was just telling stories and not telling them something from God. What a frustrating point in the life of this old prophet.

If the truth be known, there are many preachers who feel the same way when they are done preaching a sermon that they have prayed and labored over for hours. Many times a preacher will preach a sermon just to watch his people go out and do the exact opposite of what he just preached. Many times a preacher will give a truth to his people and then those who had just heard him preach that truth come and ask counsel of him about the very thing that he has just preached. How frustrating this can become to a preacher!

We must be careful that the preaching we hear from our preacher doesn't become just another sermon or a great story that he is telling us. We must be careful that we don't become blank faced as the preacher preaches and let our minds wander as he is giving us a truth that he feels will help us.

Have you become guilty of this? You must understand that a preacher gives his life to help you through the preaching, and then for you not to listen can become very frustrating to your pastor. Don't be the type of person who lets the preaching go in one ear and out the other. Realize the sermons being preached are being preached for your good and not to be a *"parable"* to your ears.

Let me take this thought one step further. To every young person reading this, don't let your parent's teachings become a *"parable"* to your ears. Young people, realize your parents don't say what they say just for you to ignore them. They teach you so that you will make it in life and avoid some of the heartaches they have made and heartaches they have watched others make. Be careful that you don't let your parent's teachings become just another story that you have heard before. Listen and obey realizing they are doing this for your own good.

Let all of us be careful to listen to those who care for us and are trying to help us in life. Let us not let their admonitions fall upon deaf ears. Let us be careful not to let them become frustrated with our lack of attention, but instead make them happy that they have worked hard to help us because we do what they are preaching and teaching us to do.

When This Cometh, Ye Shall Know

Ezekiel 24:24
"Thus Ezekiel is unto you a sign: according to all that he hath done shall ye do: and when this cometh, ye shall know that I am the Lord GOD."

I was recently reading a book by a well known personality in society who was telling his story of coming back to God. In his book, he told of when he was young his parents reared him to do right, go to church and serve God. He said as he grew up that his career became so demanding that it took him away from church and serving God. It wasn't until one night when his parents were killed that he finally realized that God was trying to get his attention to bring him back to Himself. As I read this story I was saddened by the fact that it took such a tragedy to get this good person to come back to acknowledging God in his life.

The story I just told you is very similar to what we read here in this verse. God told Ezekiel that once all the heartache and tragedy came upon Israel then they would acknowledge that God is the LORD. How sad it is that it takes tragedy to get people to come back to God. You would think the goodness of God upon His people would cause them to acknowledge God in every area of their lives, but the sad part is, normally the goodness of God upon our lives causes us to focus on what His goodness has given to us instead of God.

I wonder as I write this, how many people who are reading this devotional will have to go through great tragedy to finally acknowledge that God's ways are right all the time? I am talking to some who put their jobs in front of God in their life. I am talking to some whose careers, making money, their agendas and their own hobbies have become more important to them than God. Is God going to have to bring great tragedy upon your life to finally get you to look back to Him? No, I am not saying you are living a wicked life. I am talking about people who are doing right, but who are not putting God first in their life. With all that God has done for us, we should be sure to acknowledge Him and His ways in our lives.

I beg of you as you read this to be sure to do what God wants you to do in EVERY area of your life. Don't let God have to bring tragedy in your life for you to finally acknowledge God's way in some area of your life. Oh, you may be acknowledging God in most areas of your life, but have you acknowledged God's ways in all areas of your life? Don't force God to send tragedy your way to get you to look to Him. Have a tender heart that wants to follow God's ways in every area of your life and desires to please Him in all that you do.

The Right Mindset Concerning the Ministry

Ezekiel 34:10
"Thus saith the Lord GOD; Behold, I am against the shepherds; and I will require my flock at their hand, and cause them to cease from feeding the flock; neither shall the shepherds feed themselves any more; for I will deliver my flock from their mouth, that they may not be meat for them."

Quite often I counsel people who are involved in the ministry. I counsel these people to help them because people have used them. I see people often who become bitter because people use them and then turn on them. Though what I am about to say may not be very comforting, my reminder to these people who have been hurt is that the whole purpose of why we are in the ministry is so that people can use us. In other words, I am only trying to remind them the reason we are in the ministry is to minister to people.

We read in this verse that one of the things God held against the shepherds of Israel was that they were using their position to get gain from the people instead of using their position to help the people. As we can see in this verse, God hated the fact that these shepherds were using the people to build their ministries instead of using their ministries to build the people.

One thing every person in the ministry must be careful of is becoming selfish in the ministry. What I mean is that we must be careful we don't expect people to give to us all the time. We must constantly guard ourselves that we don't use people for the purpose of them doing things for us. We must constantly keep in front of ourselves that the whole purpose for our being in the ministry is to use our ministry to build the lives of people. We must keep in front of ourselves the nature of the ministry dictates that people can use us.

Just looking at the definition of the word "ministry" will tell us what the ministry is all about. The word "ministry" means "to service or aid." In other words, it is all about helping others and not about others helping us.

Do you find yourself constantly complaining that the people in your ministry are using you? Well you can take solace in the fact that you are doing what you are supposed to do. Now don't take me wrong, I believe we ought to take care of those who are in the ministry. What I am warning against is taking on the mentality that people are to serve us because we are in the ministry of the LORD.

Let each of us constantly be careful that we don't misuse our position in the ministry for our own gain. Let us be careful to use the ministry for the purpose for which we are in it; to service people and to be an aid to help them in whatever way we can. We will be happy when people have used us, for when we have been used, we will have fulfilled the purpose of the ministry.

Can These Bones Live?

Ezekiel 37:3
"And he said unto me, Son of man, can these bones live? And I answered, O Lord GOD, thou knowest."

Another vision from God came to Ezekiel as God brought him to a valley full of dead men's bones. As Ezekiel looked upon all the bones in this valley, God asked Ezekiel, *"...can these bones live?"* What a question posed by God to the Prophet Ezekiel! As we look at the rest of the chapter, we see that these bones eventually had flesh back upon them and came alive.

Though this prophecy was to the Jews, I believe we can take hope from it as we serve the same God Who Ezekiel served. There are many who read this who may have messed up their lives in sin. There are many who wonder if America can ever have revival again. There are many who see churches that once thrived that now are floundering and some barely existing. There are some who read this and the best days of their Christian life seem to be in the past. I ask the question that God asked Ezekiel, *"Can these bones live?"* Can the bones of a person who has spiritually wrecked their life live again? Can a nation who was once a proud nation under God see revival again? Can churches that once used to be the lighthouse of churches thrive again? Can a Christian whose past seems to be the best part of their Christian life see vibrancy once again in their Christian life? My answer to all of these is yes!

We all have hope that as long as God is involved life can come back to those dead bones. Yes, life can come back to a marriage that has lost its romance! Yes, life can come back to a church or a nation who seems to have no hope! Yes, there is hope for anyone who will simply realize their hope is God. So how do we bring life back? Two things you will notice brought life to these bones and will they bring life back to anything.

First of all, preaching! God told Ezekiel to preach to the bones and as he did flesh came back to the bones. It is the foolishness of preaching that gives hope to those who have messed up their lives in sin. This is why we need to get back to preaching in our churches and in our nation. Back to the type of preaching that shows people there is a God of mercy that will give life again if only we will do what He commands us to do.

Second, we see it takes the Spirit of God to move upon something for life to come back to it. Not only do you need preaching to bring life back to dead bones, but you need God's power upon your life once again. When is the last time you begged for God's power on the dead bones of your life? When is the last time God's power empowered you to do something great? Oh Christian, we need the power of God in our nation, churches, marriages, homes and lives if we are ever going to see vibrancy in these areas again.

Don't ever despair if you feel that your spiritual bones have dried up in an area. As long as God is merciful and alive, we have hope that the bones can live again.

Proper Dietary Habits Are Beneficial

Ezekiel 44:31
"The priests shall not eat of any thing that is dead of itself, or torn, whether it be fowl or beast."

In this forty-fourth chapter of Ezekiel, God goes through the responsibilities of the priests in the future temple. One of the responsibilities of the priests, as we see in this verse, was to eat properly or to have a proper diet. God thought it was important enough that the priests eat properly that He gave them a diet by which they were to live. Though this verse may be talking about the priests in the temple, we as Christians must understand that according to 1 Peter 2:9, we are also called the priest of God. Therefore, if we are the priests of God then God would also like each of us to have proper dietary habits.

I am certainly no expert in dietary habits, but I do believe it is proper for each Christian to eat a proper diet daily. I want to give you some thoughts on this because if we can keep ourselves healthy, then we can serve God better.

First of all, keep balance in your diet. What I am talking about is not to go off on tangents in either direction. I have watched people go off on health food diets to the extreme that I personally do not feel it is as healthy as we all like to think it is. I believe more than going off on a health food binge we ought to keep a balance in what we eat.

Second, don't eat too much. For some reason we think we have to eat three meals a day. I am of the belief that you should only eat when you are hungry. This is where many people gain a lot of weight. They eat all the time and then wonder why they gain weight. When you are full, stop eating. It is as simple as that.

Third, if you have weight problems, keep a record of what you eat every day. This is probably where most people fail.

You may not think you eat a lot, but every little snack adds up and before you know it you have eaten more than you really needed. If you write down EVERYTHING that you eat, then you will know in what areas you need to cut back.

Fourth, listen to your body on what to eat and what not to eat. We all have some little health problems that cause us to watch our dietary habits. Study your eating habits, and find out what flares up your health problem. Whatever foods cause your health problems to flare up, stop eating them.

Fifth, have some sort of exercise routine that you do each week. I know there are people who say you don't have to exercise to lose weight, and they may be right, but I am a believer that exercise will help you in many ways. No, you don't have to be an exercise freak, but I do believe a balanced exercise program is good for your health and will help with a weight problem.

Sixth, make all of this a lifestyle change more than a diet. Let me be very frank with you, diets don't work but lifestyle changes do. Whatever diet you find is best for your health, make it your lifestyle and not just a diet.

Last of all, ask God to help you in this lifestyle change. God is interested in you being healthy, so why not ask Him to help you in this area. Too many times we leave God out of this area when we ought to include Him. My purpose for writing this is not for you to think I am an expert in this area. I simply want you to consider how this can help you. If you stay healthy, then you can serve God much longer and a proper diet can help us all to stay healthy.

In All Matters of Wisdom and Understanding

Daniel 1:20
"And in all matters of wisdom and understanding, that the king enquired of them, he found them ten times better than all the magicians and astrologers that were in all his realm."

    I believe hidden in this story we find a truth that many times is overlooked because of the main truth God presents here. In this chapter is the story of Daniel and the three Hebrew children who stood up to the king's lifestyle and said they would not eat what the king wanted them to eat. Because of their stand for right, God blessed these young men and promoted them in the kingdom. The one thing I believe we miss quite often in this verse is these young men were ten times better *"...in all matters of wisdom and understanding..."* than the king's magicians and astrologers. These young men were not ignorant young men. These young men were intelligent young men who no doubt had to work at getting the wisdom and understanding of what was going on in their day.

    I believe it is very important that God's people are knowledgeable about all matters of life. The world ought to be able to look at God's people and realize that they are ten times better in wisdom and understanding in the matters of life. Every Christian should be knowledgeable in matters of the economy, problems in society and in the handling of different matters that people often face. We must be careful that we don't get the mentality that if it has nothing to do with the church then we don't need to be knowledgeable in that area. Let me give you some thoughts on how to increase your wisdom and understanding in life.

    First of all, learn to be a reader. You will never increase your knowledge if you don't read. One of the greatest problems I see in society as a whole is that people don't read any more. Learn to read books that are not always easy reading books. Read magazines that deal with business and societal problems. Read the paper, and be knowledgeable of what is going on in society.

Second, talk to people who are knowledgeable in the areas of life in which you are unlearned. Learn to ask them questions about areas where you lack in understanding or knowledge. Don't be the know-it-all who talks as if you have the answers to everything in life when you don't. Realize everybody knows something that you don't know.

Third, read your Bible daily! I say this over and over again; the Bible has the answers for ALL of society's problems. You will find inside the pages of God's Word the answers to every problem our society faces today.

Fourth, ask God for His wisdom. We don't need the wisdom of man as much as we need the wisdom of God. Realize that God is the source of all wisdom, and He promises to give us wisdom if we ask Him for it.

Let me say in closing that I don't believe we need to get wrapped up in education. I believe our society puts too much emphasis on what it calls education. I do believe though, that Christians must and should be knowledgeable in every aspect of life so we can help others who come to us for advice.

Strive this week and every week of your life to learn something new. Come out of your comfort zone and stop leaning on the crutch that you just don't know anything about certain areas. Be a learner. Become a person who is ten times better in wisdom and understanding like the young men who we read about in Daniel chapter three.

Standing Is Never Easy

Daniel 3:6
"And whoso falleth not down and worshippeth shall the same hour be cast into the midst of a burning fiery furnace."

We have here one of my favorite stories in the entire Bible. It is that of the three Hebrew children who stood up to Nebuchadnezzar and his threats to bow down to the golden image that he had set up. What a sight this image must have been and what results that came from them standing for right. However, one thing we must always remember is that it is never easy to stand for right. Notice, the threat that came because they would not bow down to the image was that they would be thrown into a fiery furnace. You will also notice that they were the only three who were standing out of the thousands who had come to bow down to this great image. Nevertheless, standing and doing right was foremost in their hearts and minds, and they stood no matter what the consequences of standing were.

Today, more than ever, we need people with this type of fortitude to stand for right. Our churches need people who will stand for right even when it is hard. Our homes need people who will stand for right, and our nation especially needs people who will stand against the masses of those who are against us.

You must understand that if you are going to stand, you must stand alone. Those who stood in the past did not see what everyone else was going to do; they just stood. Those in the past did not take a poll to see how many would stand with them; they just stood. Oh Christian, stop waiting for everyone else to stand with you and stand for right on the job, in the home, in your neighborhood, for your country, among your friends and in the church. We will never change any of these if we wait for someone else to stand with us. If needs be, we must learn to stand alone.

You must also realize there will normally be severe consequences when you stand. These three young men knew what their consequences were, but they stood anyway. I warn you, if you stand there will be consequences for your stand. People will attack you, gossip about you, try to destroy you, make fun of you and will judge your motives and actions in standing. Though this may happen, you must continue to stand for right.

The great thing about standing is the result of standing. Though no man will stand with you when you stand for right, God will be there for you in the midst of the fire of your stand. Standing is not easy, but when you know you have God on your side it will make it much easier. Christian, always remember that God will not let you go through the fire alone when you stand; He will be there with you and for you.

I beg of you to start standing today. If ever our nation needed people to stand, she needs people to stand today. If ever fundamentalism needed people to stand, it needs people to stand today. Will you be one of the few who stand? Always remember that anyone can go with the crowd, but God uses those who are willing to stand alone. Start standing today!

Skill and Understanding

Daniel 9:22
"And he informed me, and talked with me, and said, O Daniel, I am now come forth to give thee skill and understanding."

Skill and understanding are two very important things we must have in life if we are going to accomplish anything of worth. Without skill and understanding, you will find yourself floundering and not accomplishing anything in life. It takes skill to know how to do something, and it takes understanding to be able to teach others your skill.

For instance, it takes skill to be able to work on a car, but it takes understanding of how the car works to find the problem in a car and teach others how to fix them. If you don't have understanding of how a car works, then you will never be able to figure out what causes a car not to work. This is why it is very important in life for everyone to acquire skill and understanding.

We find in this verse a statement the angel made to Daniel that shows us how to get skill and understanding. The angel said, *"...I am now come forth to give thee skill and understanding."* Notice the phrase, *"...I am now..."* This implies that after Daniel did something then the angel would come to give him skill and understanding. What was it that Daniel did that caused the angel to now come and give him skill and understanding? We find in Daniel 9:2 that Daniel *"...understood by books..."* This passage is showing us that Daniel studied the Bible to get his understanding. Then we find in the very next verse that Daniel set his face to seek God by prayer. It takes Bible study and prayer to acquire skill and understanding.

So, do you lack skill and understanding in life? Then why not get in the Bible and study It and spend time daily in prayer? This is where you get skill and understanding. Your lack of skill and your lack of understanding in life are all because you lack time studying the Bible and time in prayer. The skill and understanding I am talking about is the skill and understanding of life itself. You can have skill and understanding about many other things, but without skill and understanding in life you will not go too far and you will not be able to help many people. Every day of your life you need to spend time studying the Bible and spend time seeking God in prayer. If you do this, God will give you the skill and understanding you need for life. You will be pleasantly surprised when you do this how God will come through for you and give you the skill and understanding you need for each day.

It's Not All About You

Hosea 10:1
"Israel is an empty vine, he bringeth forth fruit unto himself: according to the multitude of his fruit he hath increased the altars; according to the goodness of his land they have made goodly images."

The purpose of fruit bearing is not for the vine that bears the fruit; but the purpose is to feed others. As God talks about the sins of Israel, He says one of the sins of these people was that they were making everything about themselves; they were bearing fruit unto themselves. What can the vine do with its own fruit? Its fruit can do nothing for itself! The purpose of the vine bearing that fruit was so that it could feed others. You see, the whole purpose of bearing fruit was not about the vine. It was about others.

We need to realize that everything is not all about us. Too many times we make life about us. It is all about us getting our way in our marriage. It is all about us getting our way on the job. It is all about us getting our way in life. We have made everything about ourselves and getting our own way when God says His whole purpose in giving us everything we have is so that we can help others. When we get to the point in our lives when we realize it is not about us, but it is about others, then we will find true happiness.

A few years ago I was taking a flight from Seattle back to Chicago. When I got to the airport, I found out they had cancelled my flight, rescheduled me for the first flight the next morning and put me up in a hotel. My first response was to be irritated with the airlines. I really wanted to get home that night, but I could not change what had happened. So, the next morning I boarded the flight and the person sitting next to me was a young man who looked pretty rough. The plane took off and this young man went right to sleep. I was doing my work on the plane when this young man woke up. I began to talk to this young man and then asked him if he knew if he was going to go to Heaven. He responded he did not know and so I pulled out a Gospel track and showed him what the Bible says a person needs to do to go to Heaven. After a few minutes, the young man bowed his head and received Christ as his Saviour. When he was done praying, he told me some major problems that were going on in his life and how much he needed what I had just told him. I realized at this point that the whole purpose of the cancellation was not about me, but it was about this young man getting saved.

When you come to the point in your life when you realize everything is not about you but it is about helping others, you will find life to be more enjoyable. Stop making everything about you and start living life realizing that everything is truly all about others.

Don't Destroy Your Brother

Amos 1:11
"Thus saith the LORD; For three transgressions of Edom, and for four, I will not turn away the punishment thereof; because he did pursue his brother with the sword, and did cast off all pity, and his anger did tear perpetually, and he kept his wrath for ever:"

A great sin is shown in this verse which the people of Edom had committed. The sin was that they tried to destroy Israel who God called their brother. From the time of Jacob and Esau, God had given protection to the Edomites, who were the descendents of Esau, because of His love and desire to see Esau treated fairly and right. Yet, even though God had given His protection to the Edomites, they refused His protection and the commandment for these two nations to get along Instead they tried to destroy Israel several times. Because of their desire to *"...pursue his brother with the sword..."*, God pronounced a judgment upon these people.

All of us can learn a very valuable lesson from this story; never set out to destroy a brother in Christ. How wicked and evil it is to try and destroy someone. It doesn't matter what they have done to you. There are many times when people can do evil things to us, but this does not give us the right to try and destroy them. We must never rejoice when someone sees the judgment of God upon their lives. We should never rejoice when someone who has hurt us is being destroyed. This is a wickedness for which God will judge us. Each of us needs to learn that when someone who has hurt us is being judged by God, our response should be to pray for them.

Likewise, we should never be a part of trying to destroy someone no matter what they have done. Don't ever be a part of gossiping about someone to destroy them. Don't be a part of trying to destroy a preacher who you do not like. Don't be a part of trying to destroy a fellow employee or even a boss whom you do not like. Even be careful about trying to destroy your spouse with whom you are going through a divorce. This is wrong, and God will judge you for this wickedness.

Let us be a people who leave the judgment of God to God. When you have a problem with someone, take it to God, tell Him everything about it, and then let Him decide how to handle it.

Food Convenient for Me

Proverbs 30:8-9

"Remove far from me vanity and lies: give me neither poverty nor riches; feed me with food convenient for me: Lest I be full, and deny thee, and say, Who is the LORD? or lest I be poor, and steal, and take the name of my God in vain."

I was taking my daughter to school one day when she asked me what I wanted for Christmas. My response to her was that there was nothing that I really want. She was amazed that I did not want anything. I told her the only thing I really want is to have my needs met and God has met my needs, so I really had no wants about which to talk.

I believe that is what this verse is teaches. This verse says, *"...feed me with food convenient for me."* This person said that he didn't want God to make him full because he was afraid that the riches would cause Him to deny God. He was also afraid for God to make him poor because he knew that he could very likely curse God or blame God for all of his problems. His only desire was that God give him what he needed in life; nothing more and nothing less.

As Christians, our prayer to God should be for God to *"...feed us with food convenient for me."* Somewhere we have swallowed the philosophy that God owes us wealth and riches. Nowhere in the Bible will you find that God owes us anything but to supply our needs. If our needs are met then we should be happy. We must realize that God is trying to protect many of us from foolish living by giving us what we need. I hate to say this, but if God could trust us with riches, He would have given them to us. God cannot trust most of us with riches for we can't even be faithful to Him with what we have been given.

Let us learn to be people who are satisfied and happy with what we have. Let us learn to be people whose prayer to God is not for wealth and riches, but whose prayers are for God to give us what we need in life. We will find that when God gives us what we need in life, we will be happier than if God gave us everything that we wanted. Don't look for riches, and be careful not to blame God when lack of money is your plot of life. Just make it your prayer that God feeds you *"...with food convenient..."* for you.

You Still Have God

Micah 7:7
"Therefore I will look unto the LORD; I will wait for the God of my salvation: my God will hear me."

There are times in life when it seems as if no one understands how we feel. There are times in life when it seems as if everyone has forsaken us, and we feel like we are all alone. Such is the case in this verse as Micah talks of the remnant that are left in the last days.

Micah said in the last days that we will have to be careful who we put our confidence in, for those whom we thought would stand with us will turn against us. Micah said in these days to watch what you say to your friend, for they will turn against you. He said in these days that the family whom you thought you could trust will rise up against you. In fact, he said that you will have no person you can turn to, but then he tells us of One Whom we can look to that will never fail us; the LORD.

To many who read this, you may feel that you have no one whom you can trust or turn to, but you still have the LORD. To the spouse who feels that you have no one to turn to, you still have the LORD. To the leader whose followers have turned on him, you still have the LORD. To the parent whose children have forsaken you and left you all alone, you still have the LORD. To the person whose friends have left you, forsaken you and turned on you, let me remind you that you still have the LORD. Everyone else may forsake you, but one confidence we all have is that the LORD will always be there for us even when others have forsaken us.

When others will not hear us, the LORD will hear us. When others close their ears to our cries, the LORD's ears are still open to our cries. When others have completely shut us out of life, we still have the LORD and we know that He will still be there to hear us and to help us.

I do not know what you are facing today. I do not know what your plot is in life right now. However, I do know that if you are saved, you can go through life with the confidence and assurance that even if everyone leaves you, you still have the LORD. He is the One Whom you can count on for He will never leave you. So, take courage for you are not alone, you still have the LORD.

Art Thou Not From Everlasting?

Habakkuk 1:12

"*Art thou not from everlasting, O LORD my God, mine Holy One? we shall not die. O LORD, thou hast ordained them for judgment; and, O mighty God, thou hast established them for correction.*"

As Habakkuk testifies of the coming judgment of God upon Israel, he pauses for a bit to tell of the greatness of God. He poses as a statement the beginnings of God as he says, *"Art thou not from everlasting..."* Yes, he was reminding the children of Israel that the LORD God is not just a god who has come around lately but a God Who has always been in existence. He was testifying to the Deity of God.

You see, we don't just serve a God Who does not know what is best for us, but we serve a God Who has been tried and tested by time. How mindful we ought to be when God tells us something that is best for us we ought to do it, for He has been around from everlasting. He certainly knows what is best for us. Who are we to think we know better than the God Who has no beginning and no ending? Who do we think we are with our finite minds to challenge the God Who has made us? The duration of His existence alone demands our obedience and trust.

Then he goes further in reminding them that not only does God not have a beginning because He has always been, but he was reminding the people of God that their God is a Holy God. He is not a God who can put up with sin and iniquity. He is a God Who is holy and demands holiness of His people. Let us take a couple of lessons from this verse.

First of all, we should never worry about the veracity of God or if God can stand the test of time for He has stood the test of time because He is from everlasting. There is no other god that we should serve but the true God and that is Jehovah God.

Second, let us realize that God is holy and that we should also strive to be holy. Let us not try to bring God down to man's standard, but let us realize that God wants us to rise to His standard which is holy. Always remember that God wants man to come up to Him and that He will not lower Himself to man.

Because of this we should ask ourselves, if God is holy and He wants us to rise up to His standards, how close are we to God? Have you risen to the standard of holy living or are you still living like the world trying to bring God down to your standard of living? If your desire is to get close to God, then you MUST live a holier life, for the holier you live the closer you become to God.

Today, instead of trying to bring God down to the level of man, try to raise your standard of living by living a holier life than what you did yesterday. Realize that raising the standard of how we live will cause us to get closer to God. If you want to get closer to God, then you must raise your standard of living. Instead of trying to bring God down to you why don't you bring yourself up to God!

It Shall Come to Pass

Nahum 3:7
"And it shall come to pass, that all they that look upon thee shall flee from thee, and say, Nineveh is laid waste: who will bemoan her? whence shall I seek comforters for thee?"

I love this phrase, *"And it shall come to pass..."* We must understand that when God says something is going to come to pass that it will come to pass. It may seem at times that God is never going to come through, but we must take encouragement in the fact that if God says it is going to happen then it will happen.

If God says He will bless us if we live right, then God will bless us if we live right. I know at times we wonder if God is really listening to us and if God is really watching what we are doing. I know at times we wonder if it is really worth all of the turmoil and heartache that we go through to do what is right. Let me assure you, if God says it will come to pass, it will come to pass.

Yet, let me take this one step further, if God says He will punish us for sin, then He will punish us for the sin that we have committed. Many times we think we are getting away with the sinful lifestyles that we live, but God is keeping record and we will not get away with our wrong. You may think you have figured out how to get away with what you are doing, but let me warn you, you are not bigger than God. If God says He will punish you for your sin, you will be punished.

I don't know what sin you have been hiding in your life, but let me beg you to get right with God regarding that sin today. Let me somehow warn you that your day of judgment will come. Listen, if people like David, Abraham, Saul and many others in the Bible did not get away with their sin, neither will you. Who do you think you are that God will let you get away with your sin when He didn't let others get away with theirs? Even America must realize that God will judge her for her sin as He has judged other nations for the exact sins we have committed.

Let each of us take warning and encouragement concerning this statement, *"And it shall come to pass..."* This is a warning to the fact that God will judge us for the wrong that we do. We can find encouragement in the fact that if we do right, it will come to pass that the right that we do will eventually pay good dividends.

Pay Your Debt

Proverbs 3:27
"Withhold not good from them to whom it is due, when it is in the power of thine hand to do it."

One of the greatest mistakes I see people make in life is they wait until someone has passed away to give honor and do good to them. It amazes me how we wait until someone is laying in a casket to honor them and do good to them. Though I think we ought to be good to and honor those who are lying in a casket, we also have to remember they don't hear or see the good we are doing on their behalf, for they are gone.

This verse says that we are not to withhold good from them who deserve good. God said in this verse that when we have the capability of doing good to someone who has earned it, then we should be sure to do good to them. Every spouse needs to realize that now is the time to do good to their spouse. Do not to wait until they are gone. Too many times spouses will take their spouse for granted, and then when they are gone they want to do good to them, but it is too late. The same is true with parents and children. How many times do you see children at a funeral regretting they didn't do more to show their appreciation to their parents? I even say to parents, don't wait until your children are gone to show them that you are proud of them. When you have the power to do good to them, do it. We could even apply this to people in general who deserve honor and good. Let us not wait until they are gone. We must take advantage of the time we have with them while they are alive and do good to those *"...to whom it is due..."*

I want to simply remind you that there are many people in our lives who are due honor from us. Now if you have the means to do good to them, then be sure to pay back your debt to those who deserve the right to be honored. At the least, each of us could write a note or letter of appreciation to those who have had an influence on our life.

What you ought to do sometime this week is write a list of people who have had an influence on your life for good, and write them a note of appreciation thanking them for the part they have had in your life. If you can financially afford it, then either buy them a gift to show your appreciation or give them a small check or gift card to show appreciation. This person could be a school teacher, preacher, parent, friend, Sunday school teacher or just an acquaintance that was there for you when you needed them. Whomever it is, don't be guilty of withholding from those to whom good is due. Be a person who pays your debt to those who have done something for you in your life.

Grow Where You Are Planted

Zechariah 6:12
"And speak unto him, saying, Thus speaketh the LORD of hosts, saying, Behold the man whose name is The BRANCH; and he shall grow up out of his place, and he shall build the temple of the LORD:"

Being the sports lover that I am, one of the biggest things I hate in sports is to see a team put a lot of money into a player just to see them go to a different team and thrive. I believe that is very wrong for the team that put all the money and effort into the athlete to not be able to enjoy the fruits of their labor.

This verse makes the statement about our Saviour, *"...and he shall grow up out of his place, and he shall build the temple of the LORD."* Notice it says that the Saviour would grow up *"...out of his place..."* Though this verse is talking about the coming Saviour, I believe we can learn that He did not look for places to blossom in His life other than the place where He was planted. Let me give you a few thoughts on this verse.

First of all, stay where you are planted. If you are ever going to see God use you in a great way, you must learn to give yourself a chance to blossom where you are planted. A plant will never grow if it is constantly being transplanted. If a plant is going to grow, it must have time to dig its roots in deep. Likewise, if you are going to grow in your occupation, church, marriage or any other activity in which you are involved, you must learn to stay where you are planted so that you can allow your roots to grow deep. Wherever you are in life, allow time for your roots to grow. Wherever you are in life, dig your roots in deeply and decide to stay where you are.

Second, don't look for greener pastures. One of the things that I see quite often are people constantly looking for greener pastures instead of staying where they are. You had better learn that the pastures that look greener to you have their problems as well. Don't look for greener pastures in your marriage, for the other person you are looking at has problems just like your spouse has problems. Likewise, the other workplace, the other church and the other state to where you want to move all have their problems. Somewhere in life you must decide to take your eyes off every other pasture and decide to stay where you are planted.

Third, be sure to bloom where you are planted. Once you have settled that you are going to stay where you are, you then need to decide that you are going to bloom and bring forth fruit in that place. I am all for staying, but if you are going to make the place where you are staying enjoyable, then you need to make sure you bloom where you are planted. Growth is always exciting, and this is why you need to make sure you grow where you are planted.

I ask you, have you been looking for greener pastures in some area of your life? Why don't you decide today to stay right where you are and let those who have helped you to grow enjoy some of the fruits of their labors. Stop looking for greener pastures. Decide to stay, blossom and grow right where you are. When you settle this in your mind, you will find that your growth will accelerate for you will have now dug in deeply and your heart will be involved in what you are doing. Simply put, stay where you are and grow where you are if you want to see great benefits of fruit in your life.

Thirty Pieces of Silver

Zechariah 11:12
"And I said unto them, If ye think good, give me my price; and if not, forbear. So they weighed for my price thirty pieces of silver."

In verses seven through fourteen, God prophecies to His people about the coming of the Messiah and the suffering that He would have to go through for the sins of mankind. However, when we come to verse twelve, we also see the prophecy of Judas Iscariot selling out for thirty pieces of silver.

Imagine giving up the Saviour of mankind for thirty pieces of silver. Imagine selling out the Saviour, the One Who had helped you through life for thirty pieces of silver. You ask, how much is this thirty pieces of silver worth? It was worth approximately 113 days of the average wages of that day. In other words, Judas sold Jesus out for one-third of a year's wages. I wonder if selling out for that money was worth it to Judas? I seriously doubt it considering the latter part of the story tells us that Judas Iscariot went out and hung himself; all of this because Judas was willing to sell out for thirty pieces of silver.

As I think of this I wonder, what the price tag is on your spirituality? What is it going to take for you to stop serving God? What is it going to take for you to stop selling your life out to God? What is your thirty pieces of silver? It is easy to say that we will never sell our Saviour out for anything, but the truth of the matter is I have seen many a person sell out for many different things. For instance, I have seen people sell their Christianity out for a raise on the job that takes them out of church. I have seen people sell out their Christianity for the sake of a promotion that would move them away from a good Bible-believing church. I have seen people sell out their stand for the old-time religion for the sake of being accepted by the modern day religious movement. I have seen people sell out their purity for the sake of five minutes of pleasure. What is the price tag you will place on your Christianity, purity or your stand for the old-time religion? What will it take for you to give these up?

I hope as you read this that you will determine inside yourself that you will not put a price tag on what you believe. I hope that somehow this little challenge will motivate you to take a stand for right and decide never to sell out for your thirty pieces of silver. Your Saviour is of far more value than thirty pieces of silver. Your testimony is of far more value than thirty pieces of silver. The fundamentals of the faith are of far more value than thirty pieces of silver. Even our nation is of far more value than thirty pieces of silver.

If you are never going to sell out, then you will have to be ready to suffer because most who sell out do it for the sake of comfort and ease. Those who never sell out realize there will be hard times that they will endure, but at least they can look in the mirror and say, "I never sold out for thirty pieces of silver." Be that one, who at the end of your life, can say that you never sold out. You never had a price tag on what you believed. If you ever come to the point when you must choose, then look at the end of Judas Iscariot's life and ask yourself if that is the end you want. Selling out for thirty pieces of silver will bring you the same end of self-worthlessness.

Opening Heaven's Windows

Malachi 3:10
"Bring ye all the tithes into the storehouse, that there may be meat in mine house, and prove me now herewith, saith the LORD of hosts, if I will not open you the windows of heaven, and pour you out a blessing, that there shall not be room enough to receive it."

Inside this verse I see a wonderful prayer promise that God gives to every person who will follow this verse's instructions. Have you ever come to a point in your life when it seemed as if there were iron gates between you and God? I mean, have you ever thought that your prayers were hitting the ceiling and that God was just not listening to you? Let me show you what God says to do in order to open the windows of Heaven to get your prayers answered.

I know this verse is talking about tithing; this is very evident when God says to *"Bring ye all the tithes into the storehouse, ..."* What God is teaching us in this verse is a guaranteed way to open the windows of Heaven. This guaranteed way is through giving! Christian, you say that your prayers are not being answered, try giving your way to answered prayers. When your prayers seem to be hitting a ceiling, the first thing you ought to be sure you are doing is tithing.

Now you may wonder, what is tithing? Tithing is giving ten percent of your income to God. We must understand that this is not a choice from God. This is a command from God. The great thing about this command is that when we obey it, God promises to open Heaven's windows for us, to not only get answered prayers, but to also get blessings from God that we will not have enough room to receive them all.

However, I believe a principle that God is teaching in this verse goes even further. I believe the principle that God is teaching is that giving in general opens Heaven's windows. I am talking about giving of your time to help others. I am talking about giving possessions to others. I am talking about giving money above your tithes to help others or even your church. God says that giving is a guaranteed way to open Heaven's windows.

Doesn't it seem that those who are the most involved in the Christian life seem to get the most answered prayers? There is a reason for this. They are giving, and giving is the thing that gets God's attention so that He will open up His windows to hear that person. When a person gives of themselves to God, God is going to be sure they have the best line open to Him to get things to help them as they serve others. You see, the key to opening Heaven's windows is giving.

Do you need Heaven's windows opened in your prayer life? Make sure you are tithing, and then try giving to others. This is God's guaranteed method of you opening a prayer line to Him. Giving is a way that we can be sure that God will hear our prayers. Try giving to someone today and see if you don't get a prayer answered. Try getting involved in a ministry of your church that causes you to give of yourself and see if you don't get more prayers answered. The more you give, the more Heaven's windows will be open to your prayers.

Casting and Mending

Matthew 4:18
"And Jesus, walking by the sea of Galilee, saw two brethren, Simon called Peter, and Andrew his brother, casting a net into the sea: for they were fishers."

Have you ever wondered what Jesus saw in His disciples that would cause Him to call them to follow Him? If you have, I believe you will find the answer in verses 18 and 21 of this chapter.

In verse 18, Jesus is walking by the Sea of Galilee, and the Bible says that Jesus saw Peter and Andrew *"...casting a net into the sea..."* Then we go to verse 21, again Jesus was walking by the same sea, and He comes upon James and John, but the Bible states about them that they were *"...mending their nets..."* It is interesting that the two things that Jesus noticed about these men both had to do with their nets.

In the Christian life, one of the things that God wants all of us to do is to be fishers of men; we call this being soul winners. God is interested in using people who are concerned about the souls and lives of others. Notice, the first thing that caught the attention of Jesus is that they were casting their net. If you expect to be used of God, then you must be a person who goes after the souls of men to see them saved. You must be a soul winner! Listen, people are going to Hell, and we must be aggressive about seeing people saved. Why were these men casting their net? Because they knew, if they did not go after the fish, that the fish would not jump into their net. Likewise if we don't go after people, people will not just jump in and get saved. Someone must go after them for them to realize their need of a Saviour.

Yet, not only must we go after the souls of men, we must continually mend our nets so we can reach more people. Now I believe we can look at this in two ways. First, if we are going to be the fishers of men that we need to be, we must continually work on cleaning up our lives so we have a better testimony to reach people. Yes, we can reach people even if we have sin in our lives, but we can reach more people if we have less sin in our lives. If our nets or our lives need some mending from sin, then get rid of the sin so you can reach more people for Christ. We should constantly be working on the mending of our lives so we can reach more people.

Second, I think this mending of the nets can show us that once we get people saved we need to work on helping them to mend their lives so they can also reach people. Your job is not done when you led them to Christ. Yes, glory to God they are saved! However, once they are saved, we must now work with them to see them clean up their lives so that we can send them back out to reach people for Christ themselves.

Today, let us realize that the way we are going to reach people is by casting and mending our nets. These two things will catch the eye of the Saviour which will cause Him to want to use us more. Find someone today who is lost and lead them to Christ. Think of someone today who you can help to mend their life so they can see someone saved. If you do see someone saved, then email me and tell me about the one whom you led to Christ.

Are You Worthy?

Matthew 10:38
"And he that taketh not his cross, and followeth after me, is not worthy of me."

We hear quite often people say that they are not worthy to be a Christian. On the surface this sounds correct, for the truth is all of us are just a bunch of sinners who are saved by the grace of God. Biblically, this is not a correct statement. Jesus says in this verse that we can be worthy of Him if we will do one thing, take up our cross and follow Him. So what is this cross that we must take up so that we can be worthy?

When you take this whole passage of Scripture in context, you read that Jesus is talking about His disciples being willing to choose Him over any thing else including family and friends. Now to take this a bit further, we should understand that Jesus is our faith. So, when we follow Jesus, we are following the faith.

To those who think it will be easy to keep the faith, I have news for you; Jesus says that the faith will be a cross that we must carry in order to keep it. It is never easy to keep the faith. In fact, the cross is a symbol of suffering and loneliness. Jesus was teaching us that if we are going to keep the faith and follow Him that it is not going to be easy to do so. To keep this faith will cost many of us our relationships with family and friends. To many of us it will cost us suffering and heartache, this is why Jesus compared this to carrying a cross.

Now to those who are not willing to carry the cross of the faith, Jesus says you are not worthy of Him. If you are not willing to carry the faith of salvation by grace through faith in Jesus Christ, the local church, the Deity of Jesus Christ, the belief that the King James Bible is the inspired and preserved Word of God, and anything else that makes up the faith, Jesus says you are not worthy of being His disciple.

Too many times we are too worried about what others will think of us, if we take a stand for the faith, but this is the cross you must carry if you are going to be a disciple of Jesus Christ. Too many of us are so concerned with our reputation among our peers that we will not stand for the faith. Too many are worried about the price of the battle in standing for the faith, but this is the cost. If you want to be worthy to be called a disciple of Jesus Christ, then you must bear that cross.

I ask you, are you worthy of Jesus Christ? Are you worthy to be called a disciple of Jesus Christ? Have you taken your stand for the faith and even suffered to carry this cross? If you have, then you can say that you are worthy of Jesus Christ. This cross we must carry should be carried in the church, on the job, in the house and even among our fundamental movement of believers. Let's all strive to be worthy of Jesus Christ!

Whom Say Ye That I Am?

Matthew 16:15
"He saith unto them, But whom say ye that I am?"

In this verse Jesus asked His disciples a very important question that I believe every Christian and every person needs to answer. This question that He asked was, *"...whom say ye that I am?"* At this time in Jesus' ministry, He had performed many miracles in the sight of many people, and there were rumors going around about who Jesus was. When Jesus asked His disciples this question, they responded that many were saying He was John the Baptist, some were saying He was Elias or Elijah the prophet, some thought He could be Jeremiah, while many believed that He was one of the prophets that had risen from the dead. However, when the disciples were asked who they thought He was, Peter quickly responded by saying that Jesus was the Christ.

As I think of this question, I believe every Christian needs to ask himself who Jesus is to them. To many, Jesus is just a crutch on Whom we lean when problems come into our lives. To some, He is just a great man in history who could teach us many things. To others, He is a great prophet which they can study in their religion. Yet, to some He is only an emergency number on Whom we call in our distress. To some, Jesus is a bothersome person of which they would like to rid society. To others, He is just a cuss word that they use when frustrated or irritated with someone or something.

I ask you, who is Jesus to you? Is He the friend that sticketh closer than a brother? Is He the source of all wisdom to which you run to get wisdom for the day? Is He your friend to Whom you want to talk throughout the day? Is He the Faithful One Whom you can count on that will never leave you nor forsake you? Who is Jesus to you? Is He your Redeemer from your sins? Is He your bread of life? Do you eat of His Words every day to sustain you spiritually? Is He the water of life from which you daily drink to satisfy your soul? Is He your first love and no other person's love can compare to His? Who is Jesus to you and what is Jesus to you?

In writing this devotional I want to get you to think of Who Jesus is and what Jesus is to you. Take some time today and think about Jesus. Think about what Jesus is to you and Who He is, and then write down all these things on a piece of paper. Once you have done this, then go to Jesus and let Him know what and Who He is to you. I believe if you will do this, you will find your day will be better because of Who Jesus is in your life.

Actions Speak Louder Than Words

Matthew 21:31
"Whether of them twain did the will of his father? They say unto him, The first. Jesus saith unto them, Verily I say unto you, That the publicans and the harlots go into the kingdom of God before you."

In response to the chief priest's questions concerning where Jesus got His authority, He spoke a parable unto them concerning two sons. Jesus told the story of how a dad came to one son and asked him to go work in the vineyard and the son refused to go, but later on repented and went and worked in the vineyard. Then the parable that Jesus spoke told of the father going to his other son and asking him to go into the vineyard and work, this son told his dad that he would go and work but never went. Jesus said it was the son who went into the vineyard to work that did the will of his father though he initially told his father he would not go.

This parable has a very important truth that each of us need to see. The words the son spoke were not as important as the actions that he performed. You see, God is interested in our actions more than He is interested in us talking a good talk. There are many people who talk a good talk in Christianity about all they will do, but few follow up their words with actions. Let me say this plainly, God is not impressed with a bunch of Christians who talk about how spiritual they are and then go live a life of wickedness.

Instead of speaking a bunch of words, why not let your actions speak for you? I ask you, if your actions were to speak about your spirituality, would your actions speak the same words that your mouth speaks? Would your actions and words agree with each other or would your actions condemn you and call you a liar? All of us need to be careful to talk less and do more. Many Christians talk a good talk, but their actions speak louder than their words.

Be sure that you are the type of Christian who lets your actions speak for you. Be a Christian who doesn't brag much about what you do and instead just go and do. If our churches had more Christians who would just do instead of talking about what they are going to do, I believe our churches would be growing much more than they are right now. Make it a point in your life to be a Christian whose actions justify your words.

This Cup

Matthew 26:39
"And he went a little further, and fell on his face, and prayed, saying, O my Father, if it be possible, let this cup pass from me: nevertheless not as I will, but as thou wilt."

In this verse, Jesus makes the statement, *"...if it be possible, let this cup pass from me..."* When He talks about the cup, He was using a modern day analogy of His day concerning suffering. It is said in those days that many times a cup of poison was handed to a prisoner to drink who was sentenced to death. That cup of poison was given to kill the prisoner for the crime he had committed.

Jesus, as He prays to the Father, asks the Father if it is possible to let the cup of suffering pass from Him, but notice in the last part of this verse Jesus says, *"...nevertheless not as I will, but as thou wilt."* We see that Jesus was willing to go through the suffering if it was the will of the Father.

I know that many who read this have had a cup of suffering handed to them in their lives. The truth is, many of us who have had this cup of suffering handed to us, are like Jesus and really do not want to have to drink this cup. The truth is we must drink this cup if it is the will of God for us.

We also need to realize that the cup we face was given to us by God just like it was given to Jesus by the Father. However, we also learn that there is nothing wrong with asking God to remove the cup from which we have to drink. Notice, Jesus asked the Father to remove the cup. If you have had a cup of suffering handed to you, there is nothing wrong with asking God to remove the cup from you.

The most important thing that we realize concerning the cup that has come our way is that our desire towards this cup should be that God's will be done and not our will. If it is God's will that we drink of the cup that He has handed to us, then we should accept that it is best for us and for others.

I don't know why God hands each person a cup of suffering, but sometimes it is His will that we drink of this cup. I don't know what cup of suffering you face today. It could be sickness, separation caused by death, loneliness, loss of job, paralysis, lack of finances or maybe even a child who causes you heartache. Whatever cup you face, if it is God's will for you to drink of the cup, then accept it realizing that God is there to help you as you go through the suffering.

Yes, suffering will come to most, and though we do not want it, this cup of suffering could be to help many other people just like Jesus' cup of suffering did. So, instead of running from your cup, accept it and ask God for His grace to help you as you go through your cup of suffering.

There Cometh One After Me

Mark 1:7
"And preached, saying, There cometh one mightier than I after me, the latchet of whose shoes I am not worthy to stoop down and unloose."

One of the main sermons of John the Baptist was the message of repentance. John the Baptist, as most of us know, was the forerunner of Jesus Christ and the whole purpose of his ministry was to prepare the way for Jesus and His ministry.

As John the Baptist was preaching, he made a statement in this verse, *"...There cometh one mightier than I after me..."* Though this statement made by John the Baptist was about Jesus, I would like to remind everyone who reads this that this is certainly the case for all of us. Each of us has someone who is coming after us. It could be a child who you teach in your Sunday school class. It could be a child who you bring to church on a bus route. It could be a child who you coach on a ball team. It could be a child in the church to whom you are a hero. It most definitely is your child who lives in your house. Each of us must realize there is one who comes after us whose way we must prepare so that they can do the work of God in a greater way than we do.

Now, because this is the case, we all need to be careful to make this way plain. Let us not be careless about the life we live. Realize there cometh one after us who is watching us. Let us realize, that the one who comes after us may or may not do greater works depending upon how we have prepared the way for them.

Because of this, I remind you to daily watch the life you live and be sure to make the way plain for these who come after you. I remind you to daily ask God to help you to help those who follow the path you are preparing for them. Let us always realize that our job in life is to prepare the way for those who will come after us. Then, when they go and do greater works, we can rejoice that we have prepared the way properly so that they could do those mighty works. Always remember, there cometh one after me!

Buildings Are Tools

Mark 13:2
"And Jesus answering said unto him, Seest thou these great buildings? there shall not be left one stone upon another, that shall not be thrown down."

Let me remind you of something that I fear, and if we are not careful can easily sidetrack us in the work of the LORD.

In this verse the disciples were coming out of the temple with Jesus and they made the comment to Jesus, *"...see what manner of stones and what buildings are here!"* Jesus responded to the statement in the verse we read above by telling them that the buildings they were so enamored with would one day be torn down. I believe what Jesus was trying to remind the disciples of is that the ministry is not about the fancy and beautiful buildings that we build; the ministry is ALL ABOUT PEOPLE!

All through the ages I believe Satan has tricked churches into becoming enamored with nice and fancy buildings. Now don't get me wrong, I like the nice church buildings and I believe that we should always do things first-class, but the truth of the matter is that too many times we forget the whole purpose of why we have the buildings in the first place. The whole purpose of these buildings is not for them to be trophy pieces, but to be places where we can bring people to teach them how to get saved and live a life for God. In short, our buildings are simply tools we use to help people get closer to God.

I remember one time years ago I was preaching in a church where the pastor had a different color of carpet on the platform than what he did in the rest of the auditorium. I remember a person telling me that the pastor would not let anybody come up on the platform from the congregation side because he did not want his carpet to get dirty or messed up. I will be honest with you, that is simply ridiculous! When a building becomes more important than the ones we serve, then we have turned things upside down in our ministry. All of us need to realize the whole purpose of the ministry is people. We must be careful that we don't let the buildings of our ministries become more important than the purpose of those ministries.

Every person, lay people as well as preachers themselves, needs to keep our buildings in the right perspective. Yes, let's keep the buildings we have nice and keep them first-class, but let's also not get so fancy with our buildings that people are more impressed with our edifices than they are with our purpose of the ministry. If our buildings become more important than people, then we have failed. Let's keep our eyes focused on the needs of people and not on the beauty of our buildings.

Do You Need a Miracle?

Mark 6:44

"And they that did eat of the loaves were about five thousand men."

We have the story in this verse of Jesus feeding the five thousand men with five loaves of bread and two fishes. What an amazing story this is when you consider that there were probably more than five thousand people there because God just gave us the number of men and not of the women and children. What a miracle this was! However, as I read about this miracle, I see a little outline that God gives us if we want our own miracle.

I ask you, do you need a miracle in your life today? Let me quickly give you what this passage of scripture teaches us to do in order to have a miracle. First of all there must be a need. We read in verse thirty-six that there was a need for the people to be fed. What is the need that you have right now? What miracle do you need in your life or ministry? Go ahead and say it out loud or write it down on a piece of paper.

Second, we find in verse thirty-four that if we are going to have a miracle then we need the presence of God. Oh, may I remind you that you cannot have a miracle without God's presence in your life. Do you realize that for Christians as individuals this requires us to clean up our lives so that we can have a miracle? You will never see a miracle in your life without God's presence.

Third, in verse thirty-eight we see there must be some planning. Jesus told his disciples to go out and see if there was any food. I know this sounds strange, but God will not give a miracle to churches that have poor planning. Yes, God does meet in certain circumstances, but if we want God's miracles weekly then we must be well planned.

Fourth, in verses thirty-nine through forty we learn that there must be organization in order to see a miracle. Jesus commanded the people to sit in groups which means there had to be organization. Now once you have done your planning, then you need to organize that plan. I know I open myself up for criticism in this devotional, but the fact is, if this is what Jesus did for a miracle then if we copy what He did, could we not also see a miracle? Organization is important to God. He organized this world and He organized our bodies, so why would a church being organized not catch the attention of God?

Next, we see in verse forty-one that if we are going to have a miracle then we must have prayer. Yes, prayer is the key element in miracles. God will only answer our prayers if we pray. God cannot answer the prayer for a miracle unless it is prayed.

Then lastly, in verse forty-one we learn faith must be acted upon if we want a miracle. Yes, we need prayer, but after prayer then step out by faith and trust God that He will come through on your prayer.

I certainly don't pretend to know all of your needs, but if you need a miracle today, then take this little formula, follow it and see if this is not the key for a miracle in your life, church or ministry.

Weak Leadership

Mark 15:15
"And so Pilate, willing to content the people, released Barabbas unto them, and delivered Jesus, when he had scourged him, to be crucified."

Leadership is not for everyone though everyone is a leader of some sort. We find in society that there are leaders who are great leaders and there are leaders who are very weak. Pilate was one of those leaders who was very weak.

We know the story well of how Jesus was brought before Pilate to be judged: Jesus was brought before Pilate not because there was any evil or wickedness found in Him, but because of the jealousy and envy of the religious leaders. We read that Pilate had questioned Jesus to see if He had done any wrong, and Pilate came to the conclusion that Jesus was being accused wrongly. Here is the truth I want you to notice; instead of doing what was right and releasing Jesus, Pilate allowed Jesus to be crucified because it was more popular with the people. This type of leadership which only leads based on the desire of the populace is weak leadership.

Weak leadership leads by polls and not by right and wrong. Weak leadership does what the majority of the people want them to do and not what right tells them to do. Strong leadership doesn't look at which way the wind is blowing to make decisions. Strong leadership makes decisions based upon right and wrong. Each leader who reads this must be careful to lead like a strong leader and not a weak leader.

For instance, parents who lead their children in such a way that they can be accepted by their children are weak leaders and poor parents. Leadership will not always do what their followers want them to do, but this is why they are the leaders. Leaders must realize that, at times, it gets very lonely because your decisions are misunderstood. Many parents want to be buddies with their children instead of being good parents. I have always said, you can rear your children in such a way that they will be upset with you now and love you later, or they will love you now because you let them do what they want but they will despise, and in some cases, hate you later.

Every leader must decide to lead by principle and not by what is popular. If you are a leader, the strength of your leadership is not in being a people's leader, but by being a principled and disciplined leader. Leaders who lead by principles and are disciplined in their leadership usually turn out to be great leaders. Leaders who are liked by everyone because they do what everyone wants them to do are usually weak leaders. When you study the great leaders of history, you will find that they were not always the most liked people, but their leadership brought great results.

Strive to be a leader who leads by principle. Be careful of being a leader who does what the people want you to do just so you can be liked by them. Strive to be the strong leader and not the weak leader.

Success Is the Enemy of Success

Luke 4:38

"And he arose out of the synagogue, and entered into Simon's house. And Simon's wife's mother was taken with a great fever; and they besought him for her."

One of the greatest destroyers of hard working people is success. I know this sounds strange, but when people and organizations become successful, we find many times that they stop growing, or they change what they are doing and end up ruining themselves.

As we read about the life of Jesus in the book of Luke, we see in verse thirty-seven that the Bible says about Jesus, *"And the fame of him went out into every place of the country round about."* In most people's eyes, success had come to Jesus, for He had become very famous. His hard work had paid off and now everywhere He went people would come to hear Him preach and see Him perform miracles. However, I love what the Bible says after it tells us that Jesus had become famous, the Bible says, *"And he arose..."* You see, when Jesus became famous, He just kept on doing what He had always done. He did not change His pattern of what He did. He did not change His schedule or stop going from place to place. No, when success came His way, He kept on doing what made Him successful.

If we are not careful, when success comes our way, we will destroy ourselves by not continuing the things that made us successful. I have watched churches that have grown to great numbers suddenly stop doing what made them grow and they ended up never reaching greater heights. Organizations that have become successful many times think they need to change what they are doing so they can become more successful. This is a big mistake! If what you are doing now got you to where you are, then don't change anything and keep on doing what you have always done. When success comes to you as an individual, don't stop doing what made you successful, keep on doing what you have always done; just do it in a greater way.

I don't believe people, organizations and churches intended to stop being successful, I just believe they thought they needed to change things to be more successful. Their intentions were great, but the change of their actions is what caused their downfall. Whatever you do, if in any area of life you become successful, don't change what you have done to obtain that success.

Dr. Russell Anderson, a very successful businessman who is a dear friend of mine, has told me over and over again, "It is hard to stay successful the way you became successful." I have heard him say many times, "If you keep on doing what you have always done, you will keep on getting what you have always got." How true this is!

Each of us as individuals or leaders need to be very careful that we don't let success ruin us. We must be careful that we don't let success become our ruin by changing what we have always done. The way to avoid letting success become our ruin is to keep on doing what made us successful in the first place. We will see that we will stay successful as long as we don't change what we have always done.

A Proper Perspective

Luke 7:6
"Then Jesus went with them. And when he was now not far from the house, the centurion sent friends to him, saying unto him, Lord, trouble not thyself: for I am not worthy that thou shouldest enter under my roof:"

I find in this story an amazing attitude from a person whom you would not think would have such an attitude. Here in this story is a man who is a leader, or we could even say that he was a supervisor or boss, but had a problem that only Jesus could solve. We see when this man came into the presence of Jesus, his position didn't mean anything to Jesus for we read that this man said, *"...I am not worthy that thou shouldest enter under my roof:"* Though many who held the position this man held would have thought they were equal to our Saviour, this man had the proper perspective and attitude towards himself when comparing himself to Jesus.

I believe the attitude this man had towards himself is a great test for all of us to determine how close we really are to God. When you study the Bible, it is interesting to note that anyone who ever came into the presence of God always thought themselves unworthy to be in His presence. Each of these who came into God's presence wondered why God would even allow them into His presence. Yet, as I look at Christianity today, I see people who almost think that God is honored to have them serve Him. Let me emphatically say, God does not need any of us! How honored we should be that He would see fit to use any of us. When you look at the average Christian, they have a very unhealthy perspective of themselves spiritually; it's no wonder that God cannot do many things through them. Most Christians never see themselves as they truly are; a sinner saved by the grace of God. I say this because I see people who never walk the aisle at their church because they think they haven't done anything that would cause them to have to walk an aisle. I mean, if you look at the average church invitation, the majority of people NEVER walk an aisle and spiritually this is very unhealthy.

The greatest test of how close you are to God is how you feel about yourself spiritually. The closer you are to God, the more your attitude will be like this centurion's attitude who did not feel worthy of anything from God. Yes, he wanted God to do something for him, but he realized that God did not owe him a single thing. Let each of us be careful to keep our walk with God in a right perspective. Let us realize that at our best we are still a sinner who is unworthy of anything that God gives us. If we can keep this attitude. I truly believe that God can accomplish more works through us.

Dealing with the Lost

Luke 15:2
"And the Pharisees and scribes murmured, saying, This man receiveth sinners, and eateth with them."

In this chapter we read three different parables that Jesus told when He was responding to the Pharisees concerning eating with sinners. These three parables are the Parable of the Lost Sheep, the Parable of the Lost Coin and the Parable of the Prodigal Son. I believe as you study these three parables, God is teaching us how to deal with the saved person who has left God. You will notice in all of these instances the object lost already belonged to the owner, so this would teach us that Jesus was talking about the saved. These parables clearly teach us how to deal with a person who is saved.

In the first parable that deals with the lost sheep, you see in verse six that the sheep *"...was lost."* When a Christian gets lost in the world, not on purpose, but by just getting wrapped up in the world, the Bible teaches us we are to go after them to recover them as the shepherd went after this lost sheep. Sometimes people stop serving God, not out of rebellion, but because of a wrong focus on what they were doing. This can easily happen to a young Christian who has not grown enough or in other cases people just get too wrapped up in the world and the world consumed them without them even realizing it. God teaches us that when dealing with a person like this, we are to go after them to recover them.

Then the second parable shows a lady who lost a coin. I want you to notice that she was the one who lost the coin. In other words, it was her fault. Many times we lose people to the world because of our actions and because of things we do. When this happens, we see the Bible teaches us in verse eight to first of all *"...sweep the house..."* In other words, when our actions drive someone away, we need to be sure to correct what we have done wrong first, then go and diligently seek after that person to recover them. When your actions have driven someone away, do everything in your power to bring them back **AFTER** you have corrected your wrong.

The last parable is about the Prodigal Son. The one thing I noticed about the father is that he did not seek the son, but he waited until the son came back. When someone leaves out of pure rebellion, God is teaching us not to go after them but to wait for them. You see, they rebelled and our going after them will do nothing because it was their willful choice to leave. God let the pain of this young man's choice bring him back to the father. As painful as it may be, sometimes we must let a person who has rebelled feel the pain of their lifestyle and let that pain be the object that brings them back to us. Yes, pray for them, and when they come back receive them with joy, but don't waste your time on them as they were the ones who chose to leave.

Let these three parables be your guideline in dealing with those who go into sin. If they somehow just got lost in the shuffle of the world or the ministry, then go after them and try to recover them. If it was your actions that drove them into sin, then face up to your actions, get yourself right, and then go and try to bring them back to God. However, if they rebel and choose deliberately to go into the world, then pray for them and wait for them, but don't waste your time pursuing them as they will not listen until they have experienced the pain of their actions. I hope this helps you in dealing with those who have left us and stopped serving God.

He Came to Us

Luke 19:2
"And, behold, there was a man named Zacchaeus, which was the chief among the publicans, and he was rich."

In the story of Zacchaeus, we see a wonderful picture of salvation and soul winning. Zacchaeus, who was the chief among the publicans, heard that Jesus was in town and he longed to see Jesus. The Bible states that because of the size of the crowd and his stature, Zacchaeus climbed a tree so that he would be able to see Jesus. We then learn that Jesus passed by that way and saw Zacchaeus up in the tree. Jesus told Zacchaeus to come down for He was going to his house. As the story ends we see that salvation came to this household all because Jesus came to Zacchaeus. Let me show you briefly what it took for this story of soul winning and salvation to take place.

First we see that Jesus went to the sinner. As a soul winner we must realize we need to go where the sinners are. It is the job of every Christian to be a soul winner and if you are going to be successful at soul winning, then you must go where sinners are.

Second, Jesus went to the one who wanted to hear. When you go soul winning, don't get wrapped up in wasting your time trying to convince someone to get saved. There are plenty of people out there who want to get saved. Go find those who want to get saved instead of arguing with those who don't.

Third, in order for a person to get saved they must realize they are helpless. Zacchaeus on his own could not get to Jesus. For a person to get saved, they must first get lost. They must realize that on their own they cannot get themselves to Heaven.

Fourth, there must be a presentation of Calvary. Notice that Zacchaeus climbed a tree! Can you remember another tree on which Jesus was hung? Yes, the tree was a symbol of the cross. Without people being pointed to the cross they cannot get saved, for the cross is where the sin debt was paid.

Fifth, there must be conviction! You will notice that Zacchaeus was convicted of what he had done because he told Jesus that he would restore half of his goods back to the poor. This is pure conviction. Without conviction by the Holy Spirit of God, a person cannot get saved. A person must be convicted of their sins and realize their sins will take them to Hell if they don't get saved.

One other thing you will notice in this story is that Jesus was present before salvation came. Though Jesus is not present physically today, the Holy Spirit is present to make all of these things mentioned happen. Soul winner, do not go in your power, go in God's power realizing that it is the Holy Spirit Who convicts people of their sin. The result of all of this is that people will get saved. When all of these things happen, we will see people come to Christ for salvation.

The most important thing all of us need to realize is that we must be a soul winner who will bring the Gospel to the lost so the lost can get saved. Today make it your goal to lead someone to the Saviour so they too can be saved.

Hear Counsel

Proverbs 19:20
"Hear counsel, and receive instruction, that thou mayest be wise in thy latter end."

In this verse God gives us a very wise piece of advice from which I wish everybody would learn. The first piece of advice that God gives us is to *"Hear counsel..."* I believe it is important for people to get counsel in their lives. Not just any counsel, but wise counsel. Then God goes on to say that when we get the counsel we are to *"...receive instruction..."* God is teaching us that when we get advice through counsel we are to follow that advice. That is what the words *"receive instruction"* are talking about. It is talking about following what is given to you. Then notice, the result of receiving instruction is that you will be wise. Let me point out that when you are wise you will be happy, for wisdom always leads you to the paths of happiness.

To everyone who reads this, I beg you to be a person who gets counsel and advice in your life. There is not a person alive who knows everything, because of this we all need counsel and advice at some time in our lives. One of the greatest hindrances to getting counsel is pride. It sure is hard for us to admit that we don't have all the answers, but we must realize we need counsel at different times in our life. Don't be so full of pride that you will not get counsel when you need it.

To go a step further on this subject, go get counsel at the right time. Don't wait until after you have made a decision in the matter to get counsel, get counsel before you make the decision. As an illustration, let me use a young person who wants to date someone. Don't start dating someone and then go get counsel to ask if you should date them. Get the counsel about whether you should date them BEFORE you start dating. This situation of waiting until after you have started something to get counsel happens over and over again. Though you can still be helped after the decision, you could save yourself a lot of heartache and embarrassment if you will get counsel before you make decisions.

One other thought on this subject, go to the right people to get counsel. Don't go to people who you know will give you the counsel you want to hear; go to those who will give you the counsel you NEED to hear. Don't go to those who don't know how to counsel you; go to those who have helped others in the same area in which you are seeking advice. We can always find someone to tell us what we want to hear, but what we want to hear is not necessarily what we need to hear. What we need to hear is wise counsel that leads us down the right pathway of life. Be careful that you don't run to the counselors who will tell you what you want to hear. Only go to the counselors who will be honest with you and will give you the counsel and advice that is best for you.

Whatever you do in life always remember to *"Hear counsel"* Once you have heard the counsel, then follow the advice that comes from that counsel so you can save yourself from heartache and hard times.

Opening Your Understanding

Luke 24:45
"Then opened he their understanding, that they might understand the scriptures,"

Recently I was preaching in a church where a man said to me that he has a hard time understanding the Bible. He told me that he enjoyed his preacher's preaching because his preacher made the truths of the Bible practical to every day living. Now the truth is, every preacher should do this in their preaching. However, what I noticed from the statement was that this man made it sound like understanding the Bible was difficult.

As I read what happened in this chapter, I see that Jesus had risen from the dead and was now walking with His disciples down the road to Emmaus. During this time, Jesus was teaching His disciples the Bible. Yet, their eyes seemed to be closed that Jesus was in their presence and the truths that He was teaching them seemed to be closed to their understanding. We come to the point in this verse where it says that Jesus opened their understanding *"...that they might understand the scriptures."* Throughout the three years of Jesus ministry, the Scriptures seemed to be closed to the disciples. When Jesus opened their understanding to the Scriptures we see that great works began to happen in the lives of the disciples. When you start understanding the Scriptures, then the power in the Scriptures becomes accessible to you as you apply the truths which you have learned.

Do you find yourself having a hard time understanding the truths inside the Bible? Do you find yourself reading the Bible but looking at the words and not understanding what God is trying to get across to you? You must understand that there is only one Person Who can open your understanding to the Bible and that is Jesus Christ. Without Jesus opening up the

Bible to you, you will never understand the power that is inside the Word of God.

    Everyday when you read your Bible, you should ask God before you read It to open up your understanding to the truths that He wants you to learn for that day. If you are saved, you have the Holy Spirit of God that dwells inside of you Who wants to explain the Scriptures to you. Only He can do this, and this is why we must ask Him to open our understanding. Be sure that when you open the Bible to read It, and after you have asked God to open your understanding, that you focus only upon the Bible while you are reading It. Don't let anything else take your attention like a computer, or activities going on outside your window, or people walking around the house. Focus solely upon the Word of God with your heart open to the voice of the Holy Spirit to explain the Scriptures to you.

    I believe if you will do this, you will find that you will begin to understand the Bible in a greater way. When your understanding of the Bible is opened, then apply those truths to which God opened your understanding. As you apply those truths, you will then see God doing great works in your life and ministry as the disciples did after He opened their understanding. Make it your daily prayer to God to open your understanding to the Scriptures so you can better serve Him.

Do You Believe God's Word?

John 4:50

"Jesus saith unto him, Go thy way; thy son liveth. And the man believed the word that Jesus had spoken unto him, and he went his way."

Here is the story of a nobleman whose son was sick, and apparently, there seemed to be One in that day who could help his son. This nobleman, who was a ruler of some sort, heard that Jesus was in town, and he came to Jesus to ask Him to heal his son. Jesus responded to this nobleman by saying, except he (the nobleman) saw some sign or wonder he would not believe that Jesus could truly heal his son. However, I love what the nobleman did in that he again asked Jesus to come and heal his son, for he knew if Jesus would not come to his son, he would die. Jesus then told this nobleman to go back home for his son was healed. Yet, here is the phrase that is the key to this whole story, *"...And the man believed the word that Jesus had spoken unto him, and he went his way."* It was the action which was produced by a belief in God's Word that caused this man's son to be healed.

We live in a day when the Word of God seems to be questioned all the time. I happen to be one of those who believes the King James Bible 1611 is the Word of God. Not only do I believe that It is the Word of God, but I also believe that It is the inspired Word of God. I do not believe there should be any question about this. The truth is I am not the only one who believes this. I truly believe there are many Christians out there who believe what I just said. However, what I want you to notice is that true belief in God's Word will cause action. This nobleman believed God's Word and he went home as Jesus had told him. You see, a true belief in God's Word will cause us to do what It tells us to do.

My question to you is this, do the actions of your life show others that you believe God's Word? Do your actions show that God's Word is right about tithing? Do your actions show that you believe in seeking God first? Do your actions show that faith in God pays off? Your actions validate what you say and they will also invalidate what you say as well. We can say all we want to that we believe God's Word, but if we truly believe the Word of God then our belief in God's Word will cause us to do what It tells us to do. If you believe a chair will hold you up, then you will sit in that chair. If you believe a road will get you to your destination then you will take that road to your desired destination. A belief in something WILL CAUSE ACTION.

What each of us need to do is look at our life and see if our life shows to others our belief in the Word of God. If it does, then you will have no problem doing what It tells you to do. Always remember that belief always produces action. Do your actions show that you believe God's Word? If not, then change your actions today!

Walk in the Day

John 11:9-10

"Jesus answered, Are there not twelve hours in the day? If any man walk in the day, he stumbleth not, because he seeth the light of this world. But if a man walk in the night, he stumbleth, because there is no light in him."

There are times in the Scriptures when you read a story, and though the story may be talking about something else, a principle is taught that we can apply to a different area of our lives. This is the case with the story found in these verses. The whole chapter in which these verses are found talks about the story of Jesus raising Lazarus from the dead. However, Jesus makes a statement in the middle of this story that I believe will help many to stay out of trouble. Jesus said, *"...If any man walk in the day, he stumbleth not..."* Then when you continue on in the next verse Jesus said, *"But if a man walk in the night, he stumbleth..."*

That is a powerful statement I wish everyone would see and understand. Jesus said men don't stumble in the day but they stumble at night because there is no light. What I want you to understand is this, if you want to stay out of trouble in your life, then you would be wise to not be a night person. When I say a night person, I am talking about doing a lot of activities outside of your house at night. The reason I say this is because more people get themselves into trouble at night time than they do during the daytime.

When I was a boy, my parents would not allow me to stay out very late at night because they knew I would get myself into trouble if I stayed out late. It is in the nighttime when many young people find themselves getting into trouble. Not just young people, but even adults get themselves into trouble at night.

Everyone needs to be very careful about their nighttime activities. If you are going to do things at night, then you need to be sure that these activities are planned activities with people who are prone to do right. Don't be a person who always has to be out at night. Be a person who realizes that trouble is waiting for those who do most of their activities at night. I am not saying you should never do anything at night; I simply want to caution you about doing too many things at night for this is when most people get themselves into trouble. If you participate in activities during the day, you will find that you will have less temptation to do wrong than you would if you participated in those same activities late at night.

Much Fruit

John 12:24
"Verily, verily, I say unto you, Except a corn of wheat fall into the ground and die, it abideth alone: but if it die, it bringeth forth much fruit."

The burden of bearing fruit is no doubt a big burden to carry. Many Christians out there today desire fruit in their Christian lives, but they don't desire the process that it takes for God's people to bear fruit.

In this passage, Jesus told His disciples of His coming death. He warned them that He must die for the sins of the world, but this death that He would die would bring forth much fruit. However, as Jesus told them of His death, we also find the very formula that you and I must go through if we want to bear fruit.

I don't know about you, but I don't want to be a Christian who has no fruit in my life. I not only want to bear fruit, but I want to bear *"much fruit"* as this verse teaches. However, if we are going to bear *"much fruit"* then there is a price that we must pay.

Notice the first thing it takes to have *"much fruit"* is that you must fall. Fruit does not come without failure! No, none of us want to be failures in life, but failure is part of the process of bearing *"much fruit."* The purpose of this failure is to bring us to the point where we realize we don't know as much as we think we do.

I also notice that part of the ingredients of *"much fruit"* is loneliness. Notice the Bible says that this seed *"abideth alone."* Fruit does not come from running with the crowd, fruit comes from being lonely. When I say lonely, I mean at times you will be misunderstood because of your desire for fruit. There will be times when people will forsake you in your pursuit of fruit. We must face it; if we are going to bear fruit, then it will be a lonely journey. If you cannot take loneliness, then you will never bear *"much fruit."*

There is another ingredient to bearing *"much fruit,"* and that ingredient is death. Notice again that the seed had to die in order to bear fruit. If you are going to be a Christian who bears *"much fruit"*, then you must be a Christian who dies to self. You must die to your desires and accept the desires that God has for you. You must die to worldly pleasures and accept the pleasures of God. You must die to your own emotions and pursuits of life and accept the plot of life that God has for you.

These are the ingredients to bearing *"much fruit."* I ask you, do you still want to bear *"much fruit?"* If you do, and this should be the desire of every Christian, then you must be ready for failure to come or loneliness to be a part of your life and be ready to die to self. Without these, you will never see *"much fruit"* in your Christian life. Don't settle in your Christian life for just bearing fruit; determine today to be a Christian who bears *"much fruit."* Be ready though when you determine to bear *"much fruit"* to go through the process necessary to bear this fruit.

Do You Really Know Them?

John 14:9

"Jesus saith unto him, Have I been so long time with you, and yet hast thou not known me, Philip? he that hath seen me hath seen the Father; and how sayest thou then, Shew us the Father?"

Jesus is coming down to the end of His ministry on Earth and knows that His death is imminent. As He gave His final instructions to the disciples, He told them that if they knew Him then they have known the Father as well. Philip in response to this statement asked Jesus to show them the Father. Jesus responded by saying, *"...Have I been so long time with you, and yet hast thou not known me, Philip?..."* What Jesus was asking Philip was, if he had caught what Jesus had taught him all these years, or did he just waste the time that Jesus was in his presence? What a thought provoking question!

For several years, I served under the ministry of one of the greatest pastors of our generation, Dr. Jack Hyles. I remember when he passed away many preachers would say, "Have you caught what he taught?" They were asking people if they learned from him everything that he taught or were they so enamored with his presence when they were around him that they never heard his teachings and preaching.

I wonder as you read this, who is it that you are not catching what they are teaching you? Like Jesus said to Philip, do you really know the person whom you have been around for such a long time or are you wasting your time with them by not learning what they are trying to teach you? Are you learning from your pastor who teaches and preaches to you each week, or are you just letting what he preaches go in one ear and out the other? For instance, do you even know what your pastor preached last week?

Children, have you been around your parents your whole life and yet have not caught what they are trying to teach you? Are you so wrapped up in yourself that your parent's teachings are just a bunch of words to which you don't listen? To the married person, have you been with your spouse for such a long time and yet you do not know them? Do you even know what they are trying to accomplish in life? The truth is that person will one day pass away. When they are gone, you will wish that you had taken advantage of every opportunity you had to know them better and learn from them.

When you are at church, LISTEN to what your preacher is preaching so that you can catch what he is trying to teach you. When you are around your parents, OBSERVE what your parents are trying to get you to do with your life. Married couples – get to know each other better. Stop being so wrapped up in your computer, email and hobbies, that your spouse never sees you because you are ALWAYS doing your own thing. I am afraid that many people are one day going to regret that they did not know the people whom they were around all the time and will end up regretting the time they wasted.

Don't just be with those whom you spend time, rather get to know them. Learn who they are and what they are trying to teach you so that when they are gone, you will be able to look back and say that you caught who they were and what they taught.

What He Really Said Was...

John 21:23
"Then went this saying abroad among the brethren, that that disciple should not die: yet Jesus said not unto him, He shall not die; but, If I will that he tarry till I come, what is that to thee?"

We read in the last verses of the book of John a conversation between Jesus and Peter. Peter asked the Saviour about the one who betrayed Him, and Jesus gave no response. Then Peter, probably being a little nervous in the presence of Jesus in His glorified body, saw John near Jesus and asked Him what John should do. Jesus responded to this statement, but the response is not what I want you to notice. What I want you to notice is the reaction of those who heard Jesus' response. Their reaction was to read into the statement and then they started spreading what they read into it. Notice though, what these people thought was being said was not what the statement really meant. So, because they misunderstood a statement, a false report of what Jesus said was being spread. We must be careful about trying to read into what a person really means when they make a statement.

Have you ever been around people who say, "What do you think he meant by that statement?" How foolish it is to try and read someone's intentions by reading into what they say. What is wrong with just taking what they said at face value? We have become a society that thinks when a person says something that they really meant more than what they said. We need to be careful about thinking like this.

Most of the time when we read into someone's statement, we are either trying to take their statement to prove that our own agenda is right or we are trying to use their words so we can attack them. Either is wrong! If someone is trying to say more in a statement than what they really said, then let them be the one who explains fully what they really meant. Until then, be careful about reading into someone's statement and then spreading what you interpreted as fact. You could find yourself being greatly embarrassed if you continue this practice. The safest thing you can do is take what people say at face value.

Let me take this one step further; don't you become a person who doesn't say what you mean. What I mean by this is, when you speak to people, say what you mean and don't try to covertly hide your meaning in your statements. If you say what you mean plainly, then you will find that people will know what you meant. Just like Jesus in this statement; He said what He really meant. Those around Him took the statement wrong. However, in the majority of Jesus' statements, people never walked away wondering what He really meant.

Be the type of person who speaks plainly and says what they mean, and also, be the type of person who takes what people say at face value. If you don't understand what someone said, then ask them, so they can clearly tell you what they said and what they meant.

Watch Yourself When You Disagree

Acts 5:35
"And said unto them, Ye men of Israel, take heed to yourselves what ye intend to do as touching these men."

When it comes to life and people getting along with each other, there are sure to be times when we will disagree with one another. Because we are all sinners, everyone cannot be right all of the time, and most certainly, we ourselves will never be right all of the time because we are sinners as well.

Gamaliel, a very wise man, knew there was some definite disagreement between Peter and the religious leaders of his day. These religious leaders wanted to kill Peter and Gamaliel warned them to *"...take heed to yourselves what ye intend to do as touching these men."* He was teaching them to be very cautious in their response to their disagreement with Peter because they didn't want to be on the wrong side of this issue.

Each of us will have disagreements with others. These disagreements will happen in our marriages, churches, jobs, the political spectrum and with people in general. When these disagreements come, we must be careful how we conduct ourselves through the disagreement. That is what was being said when Gamaliel told these men to *"...take heed to yourselves..."* He was telling them to be careful in handling their disagreement.

When you have a disagreement with someone, first of all move slowly in your response. Don't ever be quick to respond to a disagreement. Realize that swiftness in a disagreement can lead to a decision based upon emotion which, most of the time, will lead to wrong decisions.

Next, realize that you could be wrong. Too often we think we are always right. I have news for you; you are not always right because you are not God. Therefore, because you are not always right, you could be wrong on this issue that you disagree on. So, when disagreement comes, give the other side a chance to explain themselves before you determine your response or action.

Next, be sure you have the Bible on your side before you respond. Don't find yourself fighting over things that are preferences. Most of the time people fight and squabble over preference more than they fight over right and wrong. You had better be sure the Bible is clear in what you believe before you start using It as your source of facts.

Next, don't kill a flee with a bomb. What I mean by this is many times we want to take care of a small matter by attacking everyone. This is not the way God would have us to deal with matters. If I can settle a matter and salvage a person, then that is what I want to do. I don't want to attack the person. I want to deal with the wrong and leave the person's dignity in tact so they will respect me in my future dealings with them.

Next, deal with the person whom you have the disagreement with in such a way that you can work with them later on if they change. You need to work through the disagreement in a way that you leave space so that the both of you can work together in the future. I have seen many times, when disagreements are trying to be settled, that the disagreement is handled in such a way that both sides could never work with each other in the future. They could have worked with each other if they would have handled the disagreement correctly realizing that they might be on the same side again sometime in the future.

Last of all, when the disagreement is not settled, don't live the rest of your life trying to destroy the person with whom you disagree. Don't make the disagreement personal! Agree to disagree and move on in life. If we all learn to handle disagreements in this manner, I believe we will find ourselves learning to get along more with others, which should be a goal of every Christian.

The Most Important Duties of the Church

Acts 6:4
"But we will give ourselves continually to prayer, and to the ministry of the word."

As the church in Jerusalem grew, so did the outside business duties of the church. Church growth is exciting, but it can also be hard to keep up with all the hospital calls, counseling sessions, building up-keep and regular business duties that are required for the church to stay in existence. The church of Jerusalem was experiencing this and it was pulling the Apostles away from their main duties in the ministry which were prayer and the preaching of the Word of God. The Bible teaches us that because this happened, they appointed deacons in the church to help with the business matters of the church so that the leadership could still do the most important duties in the church: prayer and preaching the Word of God.

Every church needs to be careful that they don't let the most important duties of the church suffer because they spend more time in the business matters of the church. I know, most people would think this devotion is only for the preachers, but the truth of the matter is, this is for every Christian who is involved in the work of the church. I am not against the ministries that our churches have, but if we get so busy in all the ministries that we don't have time to pray, study the Word of God and go soul winning, then we are too busy.

It is amazing that everyone would acknowledge that prayer, Bible study and soul winning are the most important duties of a Christian, yet the average Christian spends less time in doing them than they do in all the extra activities of the church. We must realize that the most important duties of the church are prayer, Bible study and soul winning.

Let's guard ourselves so that we don't let these things slip from our daily and weekly schedule. Let's not get so wrapped up in our bus ministries, youth ministries, music ministries, nursing home ministries and so forth, that we don't ever spend time praying, studying the Word of God and going soul winning. Let's keep the most important duties that God gave the church to do as our priorities.

Let me ask you, how much time have you spent in prayer this week? How much time have you spent studying the Bible this week? How much time have you spent taking the Bible and preaching the Gospel through soul winning this week? If you find yourself lacking in these areas, then work on your schedule and be sure not to let these things slip, for these are the most important duties of the church, and your Christian life.

How to Settle Religious Questions

Acts 15:7

"And when there had been much disputing, Peter rose up, and said unto them, Men and brethren, ye know how that a good while ago God made choice among us, that the Gentiles by my mouth should hear the word of the gospel, and believe."

As Paul and Barnabas taught the people in Antioch the Bible, we find some men from Judaea came and tried to teach that circumcision was part of salvation. According to the Bible, this teaching caused an argument in the church to the point where Paul and Barnabas were sent back to the church of Jerusalem to find out what the rest of the Apostles believed and taught. As Paul and Barnabas told the church in Jerusalem of this teaching, we see that the Pharisees in this church thought this was a good thing to teach along with salvation. However, as the question was causing a considerable amount of discussion and dissension, Peter stood up and simply preached what the Bible said a person needed to do to get saved.

What better way to settle an argument concerning questions of religion; the Bible. You see, the Bible is our final authority! When questioned about who is right and who is wrong, or what is right and what is wrong, we must be careful that we don't run to man, but instead run to the Bible to see what the Bible tells us to do. Whenever you have a question about what to do, always run to the Bible for the answer.

I have heard preachers defend what they believe by saying, "The Baptist position has always been..." Now the truth is I am a Baptist and I don't apologize for being a Baptist, but just because the Baptist position has always been something does not always make it right. For instance, there have been Baptists in the past who believed things that were wrong. Just because they are Baptist does not make them right. My final authority and your final authority is the Bible.

When a certain position disagrees with what the Bible plainly states, then the Bible is always to be followed over that position.

Let each of us run to the Bible when we have questions instead of running to books or man. Don't be guilty of running to books when you have The Book, which is the King James Bible 1611. Always remember one thing; the Bible is our final authority; not a man or his position, only the Bible!

Watch and Remember

Acts 20:30-31

"Also of your own selves shall men arise, speaking perverse things, to draw away disciples after them. Therefore watch, and remember, that by the space of three years I ceased not to warn every one night and day with tears."

As Paul readies the church of Ephesus for his departure, he gives them warning that after he is gone men will come into the church and try to destroy the church with false doctrine. The first group that he warned them about was outside people who would care less about the church. He said these men would come in like wolves and would destroy the church. Then he said there was another group that will destroy the church, and that group will come from within. He said this group will come from their own congregation. This group will twist things that are said so they can get their own following and then draw people away from the truth. As Paul concludes, he warns them to watch for these people and remember what they had been taught from the Word of God so they don't become one of those who leave the church.

I write this for one purpose, to warn each of us about those who can destroy us and lead us away. I believe the most dangerous type of people who can lead us astray are those whom we know and trust. Notice, Paul said that some of those who will draw the disciples away will come from within. No doubt these men were leaders in the church. These types of people are so dangerous because we trust them and what they teach. We have heard them preach for years. We have gone to their conferences and supported them. Because of this, we have given them our trust. However, if we are not careful, we will give them our blind trust and then they will teach something that is against the Word of God and will lead us away.

Let me say very bluntly, NOBODY deserves our blind trust. Everybody's sermons and teachings must be tested by the

Word of God. If someone we trust teaches something that is contrary to the Word of God, then we have a responsibility to stop following them. If we continue to follow them as they go astray, we will also lead others astray who follow us.

I remember years ago as I was talking to my pastor, we were talking about men who have changed over the years. He looked at me and told me that none of us are guaranteed that we will never change. Then he made the statement to me, "Bro. Domelle, I don't know that you will be the same in twenty years as you are right now, for I have seen better men than you change." What a sobering statement this was to me as he warned me that even the best of men can change.

Because of this, we must take Paul's warning to the church to watch and remember. We must watch what men preach and teach, remember what the Bible teaches, and make sure that what is being taught and preached coincides with the Word of God. If it does not, and they continue to teach and preach error, then we must make our stand and not follow such men.

Again, NOBODY deserves blind trust other than Jesus Christ! So, when men begin to teach something in error and continue to preach that error, let us watch and remember what we have been taught from the Word of God. We should leave such men realizing that truth is more important than any personality that we may follow.

For What Are You Known?

Acts 21:28
"Crying out, Men of Israel, help: This is the man, that teacheth all men every where against the people, and the law, and this place: and further brought Greeks also into the temple, and hath polluted this holy place."

While Paul was observing the Jewish vow, the people that took him said, *"...This is the man, that teacheth all men every where..."* What I enjoy about this statement is that Paul was not known for anything else other than being one who teaches the truths of God's Word everywhere he went. What a thing for which to be known!

However, as I think of this, I wonder what is it you are known for? What is it on the job that people know you for? What is it in your neighborhood that people know you for? What is it in your house that your family knows you as? The truth is, sometimes people know us for something far different than what we know ourselves. If this same crowd which accused Paul were to see you, would they say the same thing about you as they said about Paul, or would they know you as one of their buddies who runs with them no matter what they do? Each of us needs to be careful what we are known for in each place that we frequent. Let me quickly give you a couple of things for which I believe you ought to strive to be known.

First of all, be known as a Christian. Don't hide that you are a Christian. Everywhere you go you should let people know that you are saved and on your way to Heaven. Don't be ashamed of this, but let people everywhere know about this.

Second, be known as a person who is honest. I believe everyone should strive to be known as a person of their word. You should never want people to say about you that you can't be trusted because you never follow through on what you say, or you say one thing but do something different.

Third, be known as a soul winner! People should know one thing about you like they did about Paul and that is you witness everywhere you go. Witnessing everywhere you go is not a real hard thing to do. I believe you can do this if you simply are not ashamed to let people know you are a Christian.

Last of all; be sure people know you as a good person. When I say good person, I mean someone who does right all the time. You should never be known as the person who skirts the rules or the person who is the troublemaker. You should want people to know you as a person who does right to the best of your capability.

Though I know there are many other things that we could discuss on a topic like this, I simply want to remind you of a few important things that I believe we all should strive to be known as. Strive to be like Paul, and be a person who is known for good things.

Don't Be a Know-It-All

Acts 27:11

"Nevertheless the centurion believed the master and the owner of the ship, more than those things which were spoken by Paul."

As a boy growing up, and even as a young man listening to older preachers, I was always taught that everybody knows something that I do not know. Hence, because everybody knows something that I do not know, everybody then becomes my teacher.

In this verse, the centurion was responsible for making sure the prisoners got to the destination to which they were headed for the trial of their crimes. As they were about ready to set sail, Paul who was a prisoner, warned the centurion that harm was ahead and that they should just stay put until the danger was over. The centurion thought he would rather listen to the shipmaster over Paul, as you can imagine, Paul was just a prisoner. This centurion was probably thinking that this prisoner just wanted to delay his trial. Instead of listening to Paul, they set sail and the ship ended up wrecking because of the storm. This centurion would have saved himself a lot of trouble if he would have realized that everyone knows something that he does not know.

We must be careful that we don't become a know-it-all in our area of control. It can be very easy as a leader to think that those underneath us don't know what they are talking about. If pastors are not careful, they can get to the point where they think their church members don't know what they are talking about and they stop listening to them. Parents can get to the point where they never listen to their children and what their children think should be done. Those in management positions in the workplace can think that because they hold position they don't need to listen to those underneath them. Even in the armed forces, those who hold rank can sometimes get to the point where they never listen to those who are out in the field facing the battle. When a person gets to the point where they never listen to those underneath them, then they have come to a point in their life when they are sure to make detrimental decisions.

Let's be careful not to become a know-it-all! Each of us should take the suggestions of those underneath us seriously and consider them for they may be right. Just because the suggestion came from someone beneath us does not mean that it is not right. Everyone knows something that we do not know. Everyone can see something that we cannot see. Because of this, we must learn to listen to those who give us suggestions realizing that their suggestion just may keep us from making a hurtful decision because often they can see things from a different perspective than we do. Let's learn to listen and strive not to be a know-it-all.

Sin's Lie

Romans 7:11
"For sin, taking occasion by the commandment, deceived me, and by it slew me."

In this chapter of the book of Romans, Paul was dealing with sin and the law. He was teaching that the law is what shows us what sin is. Without the law, we would not know what is and what is not sin.

However, as you come to the verse above, you will notice that sin is a liar. Notice the verse says that sin *"...deceived me..."* Sin always paints a pretty picture, but sin never delivers the goods it promises. The reason for this is that sin is a deceiver. Not only is sin a deceiver, but you will also notice in this verse that sin's end is always death. Notice the phrase, *"...and by it slew me."* He was saying that sin deceived him and did not give him what it promised, instead what sin gave him was death.

Oh, how every person needs to realize the importance of this truth. Every person needs to realize that sin is a liar, and sin will not give you what it promises you. No, instead it gives you death. Instead it kills and destroys everything that you know as good in your life.

I don't know what sin is offering you today, but whatever it offers you, it is a lie. If sin is offering you an adulterous affair, let me simply warn you that it will not give you what you want. It will destroy your relationship with your spouse. It will destroy the relationship you now have with your children. If sins offer is material success if you will simply put your church attendance aside, I warn you, this is a lie. You may think that missing church for your job will not hurt you, but let me warn you, for years the sin of materialism has destroyed families, marriages and happiness. It never gives you what it promises!

I don't know what sin is offering you today, but let me warn you, this offer is a deception. This offer will not bring what you think it will bring you. This offer will only give you death. Now, don't think that you will be different than everyone else. Your price tag on sin is the same as everyone else's price tag, and you will have to pay it whether you like it or not. Today, as sin offers its bargains to you, please, whatever you do, reject those offers and strive to live a holy life.

Getting Along with People

Romans 12:18
"If it be possible, as much as lieth in you, live peaceably with all men."

One of the hardest endeavors that you will ever accomplish in life is that of getting along with people. Let's face it, getting along with people wouldn't be so hard if there were no people. However, the fact is, there are people and we must get along with them.

The Bible commands us in the verse above that with all of our being we are to do our best to *"...live peaceably with all men."* Now notice, it does not say to *"live peaceably"* with whom it is easy to get along. No, in fact God deals with getting along with those who are NOT easy to get along with. Anybody can get along with people who are easy going, but it is those who seem to be obstinate and difficult that makes the command of this verse so hard. Let's face it, sometimes our boss is not easy to get along with. Sometimes our neighbors are not easy to get along with. Sometimes our spouse is not easy to get along with. Sometimes our siblings are not easy to get along with. Even at times our parents are not easy to get along with. People in general are hard to get along with at times depending upon what mood you catch them in that day. Now we must learn to get along *"...with all men..."* even those who are hard to get along with. How do we get along with those who are not the easiest people to get along with?

First, don't react according to the actions of others. God commands us to *"Recompense to no man evil for evil."* The word *"recompense"* means *"to compensate."* In other words, God wants us to realize that if we are going to get along with people, we must not act like them. We must do right whether or not they do right.

Second, predetermine to treat people properly. That is what God was teaching us when He told us to *"Provide things honest in the sight of all men."* The word *"provide"* is in the future tense implying that before someone acts, we must determine to not react according to their actions. You will never get along with people if you don't predetermine how you are going to treat people when they treat you in a bad way.

Third, don't live to get revenge. You will never get along with people if you live your life trying to get revenge with those who do you wrong. You must realize that vengeance belongs to God and not to man.

Fourth, be good to your enemies. The best way to get along with people is to help your enemies. This takes the edge off their actions. It is hard to do bad to someone who is treating you well. When someone buys you gifts or buys you a meal, it is hard to do them wrong. God wants us to realize that if we do good to our enemies, then we can get along with them.

Last of all; offset any bad by doing good. When someone does you wrong, then you make sure you do good to them. Don't let their evil actions against you make you act improperly. When they act evil toward you, be sure that you still do good and right to them.

Today, when you face that person with whom it is hard to get along, try these principles that the Bible teaches and see how much easier it is to get along with them. The more you treat your enemies right, the better chance you have of getting along with all people.

Signs of Carnality

1 Corinthians 3:1
"And I, brethren, could not speak unto you as unto spiritual, but as unto carnal, even as unto babes in Christ."

The book of Corinthians was written to a very carnal church that seemed to have more fruits of worldliness than they had fruits of spirituality. What a shame that a church would be so worldly! As Paul addressed this church in the third chapter of first Corinthians, he showed us the signs of a carnal person. Our goal in life should be not to have these signs of carnality in our lives. If we do find these signs of carnality in our lives, then we should change our lifestyle to become more spiritual in all areas. Paul shows us five signs of a carnal Christian; five signs which we should try to avoid.

The first sign of a carnal Christian is they must talk about worldly affairs all the time. Now I don't want you to take me wrong. I know because we live in this world we will at times talk about the affairs of this world. What I am talking about are people who you can only talk to about things in the world. These people never want to talk about truths from the Bible for these truths never excite them. The only thing that excites them is worldly affairs and pleasures.

The second sign of a carnal Christian is they can't take hard preaching. You notice in this passage that Paul could only preach very basic sermons to these folks because they could not take hard preaching. Do you find yourself getting upset when the preacher gets hard in his preaching? When you get offended because of hard preaching, then this is a sure sign of carnality.

The third sign of a carnal Christian is they become envious of others; envious of what others have; envious of others' position; envious of blessings that others receive. A carnal Christian truly thinks that everything revolves around them and this is why they become envious of others.

The fourth sign of a carnal Christian is they are not able to get along with others. This church was so full of strife that they could not get along with each other. What a shame! When you find yourself not being able to get along with others, then maybe you ought to consider how carnal your actions are.

The last sign of a carnal Christian is that these people are followers of personalities. What I mean by this is they will follow a personality over truth. I am not against having spiritual people as our heroes. In fact, I think it is good because if they are spiritual, they give us an example to follow. What is wrong is when you follow the personality over truth. When you are willing to leave truth to follow the personality, this is carnal. When you start fighting over a personality and not over truth, then this is also a sign of a carnal Christian.

Do you find yourself having some of the signs of a carnal Christian? If you do, then you need to grow up spiritually and stop acting out of the flesh. God's desire for you is to be a spiritual Christian. Today determine not to act like a carnal Christian. Realize being spiritual is a daily decision that we each must make and being carnal is a choice that we must not make. Let's guard against the signs of carnality in our lives.

Knowledge Versus Charity

1 Corinthians 8:1
"Now as touching things offered unto idols, we know that we all have knowledge. Knowledge puffeth up, but charity edifieth."

We live in a world that seems to think that education is the answer to everything. Consider our society and all the education that we have. If education was the answer to everything, then our society should most certainly be the greatest of all. Yet, though we have the most educated preachers in history, and the most educated society of all, we still seem to be historically among the worst of all societies. What is the reason for this? The reason is seen in the verse above.

God says, *"Knowledge puffeth up, but charity edifieth."* There is nothing wrong with education as long as we use education for the right purpose. Education gives us knowledge, and I believe life should be a constant learning center of building knowledge so we can help others. However, the biggest problem with having knowledge is that knowledge without love only produces arrogance. This is what God was teaching in this verse. Knowledge by itself will only cause a person to want to show everyone how much they know and just how much knowledge they have.

On the other hand God says, *"...charity edifieth."* In other words, the difference between knowledge and charity is that knowledge by itself is usually for the individuals gain, but charity is never for the individuals gain, but rather for the building of others. You see, charity is always about others. Charity will build the lives of children. Charity seeks to build the lives of the hurting. Charity seeks to help build up people. All in all, if a person must choose between knowledge and charity, always choose charity.

However, the best choice is this, have knowledge and charity together. The best way you can help others is to have knowledge and charity simultaneously. The charity we have can better help people if it has the knowledge to know how to better help them. Each has its own liability, but each together creates a powerful force to help people.

My purpose for showing you this is so that every day we can strive to gain knowledge. Gain knowledge by reading books, listening to preaching and by listening to others who know something that you don't know. Then, everyday add to that knowledge charity and go and help people with the knowledge that you have obtained. Take the knowledge you have and go love someone with that knowledge. Take the knowledge you have and love someone at your workplace today. Take the knowledge you have and love someone today whom you meet on the street. Take the knowledge you have and love people in general.

Always remember, knowledge by itself is vain and empty. Charity by itself will build others. Knowledge and charity together are a great team that will seek to help and build others. Today, find a way to use the knowledge that you have and love someone.

Charity Has a Blind Eye

1 Corinthians 13:4
"Charity suffereth long, and is kind; charity envieth not; charity vaunteth not itself, is not puffed up,"

According to the Bible, one of the characteristics of charity is that *"Charity suffereth long, and is kind…"* One of the things that seems to destroy marriages and relationships is a lack of what these words say. Notice that God says, *"Charity suffereth long…"* What God is teaching us is that when you love a person, you are willing to put up with their weaknesses as you train them to do right because of your love for them. When you truly love a person, you are not going to try to destroy them by pointing out their flaws. Yet, in the average church and home today we find people who are so quick to judge others and the reason for this is a lack of love.

We talk about a need for revival in our nation, and our nation does need revival. However, I believe one of the areas we need revival in is in the area of having love for people who are not quite what they should be. I believe if we have love, we would be willing to overlook each others weaknesses because *"Charity suffereth long…"* You see, love is willing to put up with many things waiting for the object that it loves to change. Love says, "I will overlook their weaknesses because I know eventually they will do right." This is what the phrase *"suffereth long"* truly means.

Let's continue on with the thought of this verse. Not only will love be longsuffering, but notice, while it is longsuffering it is also kind. Our verse says, *"Charity suffereth long, **and is kind**…"* You see, while being longsuffering with those whom we love, let's be kind to them as we overlook some of their weaknesses. The truth is you can have kindness without longsuffering but you will never have longsuffering without kindness. Kindness is part of the byproduct of longsuffering. When we love our spouse, we not only will be willing to overlook some of their weaknesses, but we will be kind to them as we do it. When we love our children, we should be willing to overlook some of their weaknesses realizing that they will eventually change in that area, but we should be kind while we wait for their change.

In your life, with those whom you work and with those whom you live, work on not being so quick to criticize people about their weaknesses. Instead, realize that teaching and training them will take some longsuffering. During the teaching and training time we need to practice kindness to those who we are trying to help. This is true love, and this is a love that God has for us. Let us be like God with others and be willing to help and train them. Realize that we must be willing to put up with some of their mistakes, and when they make other mistakes, be kind to them realizing they are working on improving in that area.

You're Not Alone

2 Corinthians 1:8
"For we would not, brethren, have you ignorant of our trouble which came to us in Asia, that we were pressed out of measure, above strength, insomuch that we despaired even of life:"

Sometimes in life it is almost refreshing to see those who are strong Christians struggle in the same areas in which we struggle. Don't get me wrong, we are not happy that they are struggling in a certain area, but we are glad to see that we are not the only one who struggles with certain things in life. This verse is one of those cases.

As the Apostle Paul addressed the church of Corinth, he told them of some troubles that had come his way. As he talked of the troubles, he told this church that he came to the point in his life that he *"...despaired even of life."* Wow, the Apostle Paul had some fear in his life. The Apostle Paul had come to a point in his life where he lost all hope that he was going to live. It is almost refreshing to know that this great Apostle had weaknesses in his life.

I say this to you because I know, how at times, we almost think that we can never become a great Christian because of the struggles that we go through in our Christian life. Let me assure you, you are not alone in the struggles that you face. Whatever your struggles are in life, you are not alone; there are certainly other great Christians who face the same struggles that you face.

Great Christians have fear, temptation, sorrow, hopelessness, worry and many more weaknesses just like you might have. The difference, though, between them and you just might be what you do when your weakness appears. When the Apostle Paul despaired in his life, instead of focusing on the despair, he put his trust in God. When your weakness appears in your life, you must not let that weakness control you. You must go to the One Who can help you through that weakness and that person is God. However, let me show you one other thing about this subject.

Why does God show us the weaknesses of these great Christians? Is it to give us an excuse not to try and conquer our weaknesses? Definitely not! Is it to embarrass these great Christians? Certainly not! The reason is to assure us that God can still use people with weaknesses. That means even though you may have a weakness, God can still use you.

Do you have a weakness in your life and you feel like you are the only one who struggles with that? Do you feel that because of this weakness God can't use you? Let me remind you that you are not alone. There are probably many other people who face the same difficulties you face, but they still let God use them in spite of their weaknesses. Whatever you do, don't let your weaknesses stop you from serving God.

The Purpose of a Thorn in the Flesh

2 Corinthians 12:9
"And he said unto me, My grace is sufficient for thee: for my strength is made perfect in weakness. Most gladly therefore will I rather glory in my infirmities, that the power of Christ may rest upon me.

One of the hardest things to take in life are the hardships that God sends our way that really have nothing to do with our actions. These hardships are called by Paul, *"...a thorn in the flesh..."* This thorn in the flesh is usually something that either causes us much physical pain or it is something of embarrassment that we must go through. These things are not things that we asked for and neither are they anything that God has sent our way to punish us. However, if you are going to be used of God, you will have a thorn in your flesh that you will have to put up with. So, what is the purpose of having a thorn in the flesh?

First of all we find that the thorn in the flesh is there to keep us humble. Yes, sometimes when God begins to use us, we become full of pride and God must give us something that keeps us humble. Though we don't like this thorn in the flesh, it is good for us if it keeps us humble.

The second reason I see that God sends these thorns our way is to remind us of our humanity. These thorns in the flesh are sent our way to remind us how weak we are and how strong He is. If we are not careful, we will begin to rely on our own strength and not God's, so God sends us a thorn in the flesh simply to remind us of our humanity.

Third, these thorns in the flesh are there for us to experience the grace of God. Nothing will help us grow more in our Christian lives than experiencing God's grace. I cannot explain the comfort that God's grace gives, but if you have ever experienced the grace of God in your life, you will understand that this grace is not only comforting, but it also helps us to grow as a Christian.

Last of all, the purpose of a thorn in the flesh is so we can have the power of God rest upon us. Oh Christian, if the only reason that God gives us a thorn in the flesh is so that we can have His power, then that thorn in the flesh is worth having. To have God's power is certainly the need of every Christian.

Many who read this devotional have that thorn in the flesh, and to many, this thorn in the flesh is very unpleasant. However, let us remember the purposes of why God sent us this thorn in the flesh and we will see that it is good for us and can become our friend. Don't let your thorn in the flesh destroy you, but use it to be used of God in a greater way.

Are You Filled with the Spirit?

Ephesians 5:18
"And be not drunk with wine, wherein is excess; but be filled with the Spirit;"

One of the greatest needs in Christianity today is the need for God's people to be filled with the Holy Spirit of God. I want you to notice in this verse that God does not give us a choice about the matter, but He says to *"...be filled with the Spirit;"* God wants us to be so filled with the power of His Holy Spirit that we don't control ourselves. Like the alcoholic is controlled by the alcohol, God wants us to be controlled by His Spirit. As we continue to read on in this chapter, we see the results of being filled with the Spirit.

The first result we see in verse 19 is that you will sing to yourself. In other words, being filled with the Spirit causes you to sing songs throughout the day. Now when I say songs, I am talking about spiritual songs as the Bible explains in this verse. I always get concerned for people who get annoyed when others are singing or whistling Christian songs. You see, the result of being filled with the Spirit is singing to yourself.

Then the second result we find in verse 20 is that you will be a person who thanks God for EVERYTHING. Yes, this is even thanking God for the rough times of life that He allows us to go through. Do you find yourself always complaining about the rough times and never thanking God for what you are going through? Let me put it plainly, if you are not thanking God for EVERYTHING in your life, you are not filled with the Spirit of God.

The last result we find of being filled with the Spirit is in verse 21 when God says that we will submit ourselves to each other. In other words, when you look at this verse in context, you will let the other person have their way. However, I want you to notice who God speaks to the most in these verses. He is speaking to the husband and wife. When a person is filled with God's Holy Spirit, they will find it easy to submit their will to the other person.

Let me ask you, are you filled with the Spirit? Do you see the results of being filled with the Spirit in your life? If in any of these you find yourself lacking, then you need to get alone with God and let Him fill you with His Spirit. Instead of being filled with unthankfulness, trying to get your own way in everything and having a bad attitude, empty yourself of you and let God fill you with His Holy Spirit.

Please Be Patient

Philippians 1:6
"Being confident of this very thing, that he which hath begun a good work in you will perform it until the day of Jesus Christ:"

When I read this verse, I am reminded of a song that we used to sing years ago when I was a young boy, "He's Still Working On Me." God promised us that if He started performing a work in our life that He will continue to do that work until we go to Heaven. Let me assure you, if you are saved, then God has begun a work in your life. You are the workmanship of Jesus Christ. Now, because He has begun a good work in you, He will not stop this work until you go to Heaven. Because of this, each of us must learn to be patient and not too hard on ourselves.

At times we almost think we need to be perfect or else God wants nothing to do with us. This is not the truth. We should strive everyday to be what God wants us to be, but we are going to fail because we are sinners. Now when you fail, remember that you are still a work in progress. When you are not where you think you should be, then remember again that you are a work in progress. True, maybe we should be further down the road than where we are right now, but we are a work in progress.

I have found that there are many Christians who get so discouraged because they are not what they should be. Although this is true, you will never be what you should be until Jesus comes back to take us to Heaven. Until that day, I must remember to be patient with myself realizing that I am a work in progress.

Let me take this one step further, not only are we a work in progress, but other people are also a work in progress. You know, if we would be as patient with other people as we want them to be with us, then I think we would understand that they are a work in progress and will continue to be a work in progress until Jesus comes back.

So, I say to the parent, though your child is not what they should be, please be patient with them realizing they are a work in progress. To the spouse who gets irritated with their mate, remember that your mate is a work in progress, and they will continue to change and become what they should be, if we will just be patient. To the Christian, we must learn to be patient with other Christians realizing they are a work in progress. If we are not careful, we will run people off because we expect them to be perfect when in all reality we are all a work in progress. Even to the employer/employee, let each learn to be patient with each other understanding they are a work in progress. None of us are what we should be and will never be, but if we will keep in mind that everyone is a work in progress, then I believe we can get along with people much more easily.

So, today when that person begins to irritate you because "They should know better," remember when you want to lash out at them that they are a work in progress and you need to be patient with them. Let's all cut each other some slack and be patient with each other until God is finished with His work in our lives.

God's Will for You

1 Thessalonians 5:18
"In every thing give thanks: for this is the will of God in Christ Jesus concerning you."

The will of God has always been something that Christians throughout all ages have tried to find. In the Bible we find that there are two categories of God's will. The first category is the revealed will of God. This revealed will of God is what God commands us to do in the Bible. It is very plain for everyone to see and understand. The second category of God's will is God's personal will for your life. This will would be the place where God wants you to live; the pursuit of life in which God wants you to work; it is the area of life that you intend to do for the rest of your life. The only way to find God's personal will is to do God's revealed will.

In this chapter of 1 Thessalonians, we find that God shows us part of what is His revealed will. God made it so plain to see as He says, *"...this is the will of God in Christ Jesus concerning you."* I don't think you could get it any clearer. So, what is God's will for you?

First of all His will for you is to *"Rejoice evermore."* God wants His people to be a rejoicing people. To rejoice is to be happy, glad and joyful. The only way we can be this is to do what God commands us to do in the Bible when it comes to abstaining from sin. If you don't refrain from sin, then there is no way you will ever be able to rejoice. God's people should be a rejoicing people. This world does not need to see God's people as a people who are grumpy, sad and complaining all of the time. They need to see us doing God's will by rejoicing all of the time.

The second will of God for you is to *"Pray without ceasing."* You wonder what God's will is for your life; His will is for you to be in a constant spirit of prayer to Him. When God commands us to pray without ceasing, though it means more than what I am about ready to say, God wants us everyday to pray to Him. We should not be hit and miss with our prayer life. We should everyday, without ceasing have a time of prayer to God for this is His will for you.

The last thing we see as God's will for you is, *"In every thing give thanks:"* No matter what your day holds, God's will for you is to give Him thanks for what happens in that day. If that day is full of blessing, then give thanks to God. If your day is full of hardship and trials, God's will for you is to thank Him for those hardships and trials.

Have you been living daily in God's will? Have you daily been rejoicing, praying and giving thanks for everything? This is God's will for you! You will never be successful in the personal will of God for your life without doing God's revealed will. In this chapter, we find three parts to His revealed will.

Today decide to do God's will. Make it a point today to be a rejoicing, happy person. Make it a point that today you will not miss your prayer time. Make it a point throughout the day to thank God for everything that comes your way. Then, when tomorrow comes, do the same thing. By doing this everyday, you will find yourself doing God's will for your life.

First of All

1 Timothy 2:1
"I exhort therefore, that, first of all, supplications, prayers, intercessions, and giving of thanks, be made for all men;"

As the Apostle Paul teaches Timothy how to conduct himself as a minister, he chose to teach him about the importance of prayer. In fact, when we come to the importance of prayer, it was the very first thing that Paul wanted to teach him, for prayer is no doubt one of the most important things that a Christian must learn to do everyday.

Paul said, *"...first of all,..."* before you do anything else, be sure you spend time in prayer. However, then you will notice the progression of prayer that is taught here in this verse, which if done, will immensely help our prayer lives. Here is the order given in which we are to pray: supplications, then prayers, then intercessions, and last of all giving of thanks. Now let us look at each category to understand how we should pray.

The word supplication carries an interesting definition in that it is a prayer or petition of thanksgiving to God thanking Him for what He has done for us. It also means while thanking God, we are to ask Him to continue to keep these blessings upon us. It is a prayer asking God to allow us continued success in the endeavors that we are pursuing.

Once we finish our supplications, we are to go into what is called in this verse *"prayers."* Prayers are the asking of God for our daily needs and provision for ourselves. After we thank God for what He has done and ask Him for continued success, then we are to ask God for things either temporal or spiritual, for ourselves.

God then leads us into intercession, which is a prayer of praying for others and interceding for others. Our prayer lives should include us praying for the needs of others and interceding to God for others. Never should our prayer life be just about ourselves. In order to have a fulfilled prayer life, our prayer life must include coming to God on behalf of others and their needs.

The last thing we see is that God wants us to give thanks for all men. Notice this did not say just for those who we like and who like us and treat us well. God said for all men! This means we are to be thankful to God even for our enemies and those who would treat us spitefully. God said this is the way to end our prayers. Now why would God have us to end our prayer thanking Him for all men? God knew that if we will thank Him for all men then this will give us the right attitude towards everyone, including those who are considered our enemies.

Let us realize that when we pray this way, God says this will allow us to lead a quiet and peaceable life. When a Christian learns to pray this way, this is what will give them peace in their life.

Overcoming Fear

2 Timothy 1:7
"For God hath not given us the spirit of fear; but of power, and of love, and of a sound mind."

One of the greatest hindrances to the work of the LORD is fear. Fear will keep us from stepping out by faith because we are afraid of what might happen if God doesn't come through. Fear will keep many Christians from soul winning because they are afraid of what people may say or do to them. Fear will keep many from doing the will of God for their lives because they are afraid they may fail in this endeavor that God has for them.

As Paul taught Timothy about the ministry, he instructed him that any spirit of fear that Timothy may have that is keeping him from doing God's work or commands is not given to him by God. This would mean that if the spirit of fear is not given by God, then the spirit of fear must come either from the Devil or from us. Now the truth is, the spirit of fear usually is caused by our lack of faith in God. The majority of the time the spirit of fear is not caused by the Devil, but by our imagination that tells us what will happen if we fail. The spirit of fear does not come from God. We are taught what helps us to overcome this spirit of fear when it does come our way.

The first thing that helps us to overcome the spirit of fear is the power of God. When a person has the power of God upon their life, they will know that God can help them do whatever He has commanded them to do. All throughout the Bible we see people do extraordinary things through the power of God. It was only in the absence of God's power and the presence of the spirit of fear that even ordinary things could not be done. In Gideon's life, it was the spirit of fear that kept him from doing God's will. However, when the power of God came upon him, he did the extraordinary in conquering the Midianite army with 300 men.

The next thing that helps us to overcome the spirit of fear is love. In 1 John 4:18 the Bible says, *"...perfect love casteth out fear:..."* You know, when you have a love for people, your love for people will overcome any fear that would keep you from helping those whom you love. A parent, because they love their child, will do extraordinary things that they would not normally do unless their child is in danger. Why is this? Because their love for their child causes them to try and get their child out of harms way, even if the danger is something of which they were previously afraid. When you love people, you will find that love will drive any fear away.

The last thing we notice that drives out the spirit of fear is a *"...sound mind."* This sound mind is a mind that has proper discernment in making decisions. When you make wise decisions, you will not have fear in whatever you are doing. It is usually when you make decisions that you are unsure about that causes you to fear. When you know what you are doing, then you have no fear because you know what the outcome will be. You can only get this sound mind through the reading of the Word of God and getting the wisdom of God on your mind when making decisions.

Whatever the fear is that is keeping you from serving God, remember that the power of God, a love for people and proper decisions will drive that spirit of fear away. Don't let fear stop you from doing what God wants you to do. Overcome your spirit of fear by getting God's power, loving people and reading the Word of God.

There Remaineth a Rest for the People of God

Hebrews 4:9
"There remaineth therefore a rest to the people of God."

Do you find yourself getting tired and weary of the hardships that life brings your way? Do you see yourself getting weary in the service of the LORD? Many times as Christians we can almost become so weary in the fight against sin, worldliness and life in general that we want to quit.

I would like to remind you that this verse says, *"There remaineth therefore a rest to the people of God."* Yes, there is coming a day when the weariness that we face today will come to an end. Though we may become weary in life, the Bible teaches us that living in the will of God will give us rest.

You may think that it is not restful to live in the will of God, but let me remind you what God said in Matthew 11:30, *"For my yoke is easy, and my burden light."* We do have to carry a yoke in the Christian life, but compared to the yoke of the world, God's yoke is easy. In the book of Jeremiah, God compares the yoke of the world to a yoke of iron which is quite heavy. So, if you are wearied and tired in life, be sure to carry the yoke of God's will and you will find that yoke is much easier to carry and more restful than the world's yoke.

However, there is coming another rest for the people of God and that rest is a place called Heaven. You may be weary of this world's pressure against you to do wrong, but there is a rest for the people of God. You may be weary with the pressures of finances, but there is a rest for the people of God. You may be weary with the pressures of your job, but there is a rest for the people of God. You may be weary with the struggles of keeping your family serving God, but there is a rest for the people of God. You may be weary of trying to keep your marriage together and happy, but there is a rest for the people of God. You may be weary of fighting for your health, but there is a rest for the people of God.

Whatever is wearying you in life let me simply remind you that your day of rest will come, and when it comes, it will never end. What is this day of rest? It is a place called Heaven where we will go and live with our Saviour for eternity. So take courage Christian, your day of rest will come, but until that day, stay busy serving God and doing right realizing that your day of rest is coming soon.

Can They Depend Upon You?

Hebrews 11:40
"God having provided some better thing for us, that they without us should not be made perfect."

What a chapter, this eleventh chapter of the book of Hebrews! As we go through the chapter, we read of the great patriarchs of the Bible whom we look up to and admire for what they did in their lives. We see how many of them, by faith, stepped out and did great works for God that we can only imagine.

However, as we come to the last verse in this chapter, God makes an interesting statement about these people when He says that they are not made perfect without us. What God was trying to teach us is their works depend upon us doing our part in serving God, so that what they endured would not be in vain.

Think of this with me, Abraham is depending upon you. Isaac is depending upon you. Sarah is depending upon you. David is depending upon you. Noah is depending upon you. Enoch is depending upon you. Joseph is depending upon you. Each and every person mentioned in this chapter is depending upon you to run the race that God has set before you. They depend upon you to finish the course and not give up in your service to God.

I wonder, can they depend upon you to do your part or are you going to let them down for the sake of the world? Can they depend upon you to carry on the faith or are you going to let them down for the sake of a career or position on the job. Too many times we quit on God and quit serving God all because we have either been offended, been promoted on the job or have had some worldly lifestyle lure us away. Let me remind you that these patriarchs are depending upon you to be faithful to God and serve Him your entire life for their race to be complete and not be in vain. Whatever you do, don't let them down.

The next time temptation comes your way, remember they are depending upon you. The next time you want to quit your responsibilities in the church, remember they are depending upon you. The next time you want to miss church or even drop out of church, remember they are depending upon you. Please, don't let them down!

Everyday we need to keep the thought before us that those who have gone before us depend upon us to do our part in serving God. Keep this in mind today as you go to work, school or church. Keep in mind that those who have gone to Heaven are right now watching you and hoping that you will do your part in serving God, as they did theirs. Let's not let them down and let's be sure to show them that they can depend upon us.

Practicing Pure Religion

James 1:27
"Pure religion and undefiled before God and the Father is this, To visit the fatherless and widows in their affliction, and to keep himself unspotted from the world."

Have you ever heard the statement, "Practice makes perfect?" Growing up I heard that statement over and over again from my mother and from the men who coached me in sports. Practicing something will make you better under the pressure of the real game.

In the verse we just read, God defines for all of us what *"pure religion..."* truly is. The words *"pure religion"* imply in this verse a religion, that if properly exercised and practiced, will produce the qualities mentioned in this verse. In other words, God is teaching us to practice doing these things in order to have a pure, real and undefiled religion. What are these things that are the proof of a pure religion?

First of all, it is a religion that visits the fatherless and widows in their hard times. I love this part because this is helping those who can do nothing for you. Notice God talks about the fatherless. This is why having a bus ministry in a church is so important because the bus ministry, in many cases, brings children to church whose parents are either divorced or separated. Yes, I know that the bus ministry also brings in other children, but the bus ministry is a ministry that truly goes after those who cannot give back. This is why you should be involved in your church's bus ministry so that you can visit the fatherless.

Not only is pure religion visiting the fatherless, but notice God also talks about visiting the widows. I believe this is where the nursing home ministries in our churches come into play. In most nursing homes, you will find a widow whose affliction has caused them to be put into this home. Churches that practice going to the nursing homes on a regular basis are practicing pure religion.

There is one other thing that shows us we are practicing pure religion; keeping ourselves unspotted from the world. This is living a separated life from the world. God believes that separation from the world will help you to serve Him better. A person who goes to church on Sunday but lives like the world during the rest of the week is certainly not practicing pure religion.

I ask you, are you practicing pure religion? When is the last time you visited a child on a bus route or went to a nursing home to encourage those who live there? I know at times these things may not be easy to do, but you will never be a good Christian if you don't do these things on a regular basis.

One other question I have for you is how separated are you from the world? Can the world look at you and see a difference in the way you dress, talk and live? Or, do they see you as one of them because you dress, talk and live like they do?

Each and every week of our lives we need to strive to practice pure religion before God. Pure religion gets the attention of God. If God looked at how you have been serving Him lately, would He see a person who is practicing pure religion? Would God see you regularly visiting the fatherless and widows in their affliction or would He see you avoiding those ministries because they are not "fun?" Does God see you living a separated life or does God see you living like the world? Practice these three things and you will find yourself having a pure religion; a religion that is real.

Advice for Your Marriage

1Peter 3:8-9

"Finally, be ye all of one mind, having compassion one of another, love as brethren, be pitiful, be courteous: Not rendering evil for evil, or railing for railing: but contrariwise blessing; knowing that ye are thereunto called, that ye should inherit a blessing."

In the first part of 1 Peter 3, God deals with marriage and how married couples should treat each other in order for their marriage to work. After God deals with the husband and wife on an individual basis, He then deals with them together. In this verse, God teaches them several things that a couple must do if their going to have a happy marriage.

One of the things that God teaches is being of one mind in the marriage. In other words, God says a marriage will only work if the husband and wife have one direction they are headed together. He tells them to be compassionate towards each other. He teaches them to love each other like they would love their own family. He tells them to be pitiful or sympathetic during a time of distress. He talks about married couples being courteous towards each other.

However, the one thing I want you to notice from verse 9 is that God tells us that we are not to render evil for evil in our marriages. Maybe one of the worst things married couples can do is try to get even when their spouse has done something wrong. Let me be very frank with you, just because your spouse has had an affair or is caught looking at filthy pictures or movies does not give you a reason to do wrong to them. Many times a person will think that because their spouse did wrong that they now have a right to get even with them. What happens is the spouse that has been wronged will do something to spite the one who wronged them to show them how much they were hurt by their actions. This is very wrong! Your spouse's wrong does not give you the right to do wrong as well. Wrong is wrong no matter how you put it.

God said the way to deal with a wrong in a marriage is, instead of trying to get even, you should live your life to be a blessing to your spouse who has wronged you. I know at times your spouse may do some very hurtful things to you, but you must not act according to their wrong, you must act according to right. Right says to be a blessing even though they have hurt you.

Let us be careful about *"...rendering evil for evil,..."* Rather, let us instead be a person who when our spouse does wrong we do right realizing that salvaging our marriage is worth more than us having the pleasure of getting even. The next time your spouse does you wrong, try living to be a blessing to them and see how that blessing will do more to change their actions than you trying to get even with them.

Building Your Faith

Jude 1:20-21
"But ye, beloved, building up yourselves on your most holy faith, praying in the Holy Ghost, Keep yourselves in the love of God, looking for the mercy of our Lord Jesus Christ unto eternal life."

In the Christian life, God's desire for everyone is to build their faith. God wants each of us to constantly build our faith so that we can better serve Him and influence others for right.

We notice first of all in these verses that God commands us to build ourselves up in our faith. I want you to see that God is not concerned about building up your self-esteem or any other part of your life. God wants your faith to grow. The reason being is, the more we build ourselves upon our faith, the more confidence we will have in ourselves and what we are doing; the more proper esteem we will have about ourselves; the more self-motivation we will have and so on. When we build our faith, that faith will cause us to become a well-rounded and balanced individual.

We notice, one of the ways God teaches us to build our faith is to pray while being led by the Holy Ghost. Letting the Holy Ghost lead you in your prayer life will cause you to pray in God's will. When you pray in God's will, you will find yourself asking for the right things which God would want you to ask. This in turn will cause your faith to grow. So every time you pray, you should ask the Holy Ghost of God to guide you as you pray, and you should make this prayer time a daily activity.

Second, when building your faith, you will need the love of God to build that faith. Your faith in God is weak without the love of God in your life. 1 Corinthians 13 shows us that every talent in the world is nothing without God's love. This is why we must acquire the love of God in our lives. Daily, when you pray, be sure to ask God to give you His love, not for yourself, but so that He can love others through you.

Last of all, when trying to build your faith, it will take God's mercy. Mercy is treating another person better than they deserve. Mercy is showing kindness to someone even in the midst of punishment. In other words, if our faith is going to grow, we must exercise mercy on people who are not where they should be spiritually. This mercy will cause our faith to grow.

Notice though, all of the things mentioned that will build our faith are not for ourselves but for others. You see, the greatest way to build your faith is to live your life for others. You cannot build your faith when you live for yourself. The only way to build your faith is to live for others. This is why we must learn to pray for others, have the love of God toward others, and exercise God's mercy on others when they do not reach the requirements we put up for them. This will grow your faith.

As you go through your life, your goal should be to build your faith. If you are going to build it, then everyday make it a goal to pray for others, love someone and have mercy on others. I believe if you will do these things on a daily basis, you will find your faith being built.

What Can Wash Away My Sin?

Revelation 1:5
"And from Jesus Christ, who is the faithful witness, and the first begotten of the dead, and the prince of the kings of the earth. Unto him that loved us, and washed us from our sins in his own blood,"

What a power packed verse this is! As you go through this verse, you could literally preach on several different phrases. Phrases such as, *"...Jesus Christ, who is the faithful witness..."* Also, Jesus says that He is *"...the prince of the kings of the earth."* I mean, Jesus is not just a king, but He is the prince of the kings. This would mean that He is the best of the best when it comes to the kings. Another phrase I love in this verse when talking about Jesus is that it says, *"...Unto him that loved us..."* Thank God that Jesus loved us! He didn't just love us when we were lovable, He loved us when we were unlovable.

Nevertheless, maybe the greatest phrase for every person is the phrase, *"...and washed us from our sins in his own blood,"* The answer to what can wash away all sins that we have ever done, the blood of Jesus Christ. What can wash away the sins of a murderer, nothing but the blood of Jesus Christ. What can wash away the sins of the convict, nothing but the blood of Jesus Christ. What can wash away the sins of those who have lived their lives in sexual immorality, nothing but the blood of Jesus Christ. You name the sin; nothing can wash any sin away, but the blood of Jesus Christ.

Notice, it is not the church that can wash the sins away, it is the blood of Jesus. It is not a certain religion that can wash away a persons sins, it is only the blood of Jesus. It is not some spiritual leader of a religion that can wash any sins away, but only the blood of Jesus. You ask, what can wash away my sins? My answer to you, better yet, the answer the Bible gives you is only the blood of Jesus Christ.

Today if you are saved, make sure you take time to thank Jesus for washing away your sins with His own blood. Don't take it for granted. Thank God for that blood that washes away the sins of mankind. If you are not saved, then be sure that before this day is over that you put your faith and trust in Jesus and His shed blood to wash away your sins.

Do You Want a Promotion?

Psalm 75:6-7

"For promotion cometh neither from the east, nor from the west, nor from the south. But God is the judge: he putteth down one, and setteth up another."

In the world in which we live, we find people all the time doing what they can to impress someone above them so they can get a promotion. On the job, on a sports team, in an association, in a church, in the government and in any place that position seems to be important, people will try to be kind to those who are above them hoping to impress them enough so they will be considered for promotion to a higher position. People will even try to say things in front of those who have position just to impress them of their loyalty, so maybe, they would be considered for a better position. People will do just about anything for the one who has the power to promote them so they can get a higher position.

According to this psalm, how foolish it is for people to try and get promotion from a man when God is the One Who gives promotion. The Bible says not to look from any other place other than the God Who sets someone up into a position and also takes someone down from a position. This would mean, if you want a position then why not try to impress God the same way you would impress man in order to get that position? I know our problem is that we really don't think that God is the One Who really promotes. How atheistic this thinking is. We cannot forget that God is the One Who sets up and takes down.

I don't know in what area of life you are seeking advancement, but whatever that area is, you ought to try and impress God instead of trying to impress man. Yes, man can set you up, but God has the power to impress upon man the need to promote you into a higher position.

You wonder how you can impress God. I believe the best way to impress God is to do what He tells you to do and do it with the best of your ability. God watches how we serve Him and God is going to promote those who do right far more than those who don't do right. Just look in the Bible at Daniel, Shadrach, Meshach and Abednego who were promoted. All of these were promoted because God saw them doing right. Even Joseph was promoted to a higher position above those who grew up with Pharaoh because God is the One Who promotes. If you want God to promote you, then do right all the time.

However, just like you would brag on your boss to get a position, you should also brag on God everywhere you go. Brag on Him in your prayer life. Brag on Him to people whom you come in contact with throughout the day. Brag on Him by going soul winning and telling others of His saving power. Just brag on God everywhere you go.

So, you're looking for a better position and you want to be promoted? Try impressing God and see if that promotion will come. Always remember that God is the One Who sets up and takes down. Instead of trying to impress man for that position, impress God. I ask you, is the life you live impressing God enough that He would consider you for a promotion? If not, then change the way you live and watch God, not only consider you for a promotion, but advance you in all areas of your life.

Questions Versus Absolutes

1 Timothy 1:4
"Neither give heed to fables and endless genealogies, which minister questions, rather than godly edifying which is in faith: so do."

As Paul taught Timothy how to preach and what to preach, he told Timothy not to get caught up in preaching that leaves the listeners with questions. Instead, Paul told Timothy to preach the faith because the faith always leaves the listeners with absolutes which results in the building of their faith.

Recently I was helping a person who was struggling with making a decision about which side to stand on concerning a subject being preached. My advice to them was that when having to choose on which side of an issue to stand, always stand on the side where there are absolutes and never stand on the side of question. The reason we always stand on the side of absolutes is because God is a God Who always leaves us with absolutes. Satan's tactic is always to get a person to question what is going on, while God's method is He always gives us an absolute as to whether something is right or wrong.

This is how you always discern which way is right and wrong: when you walk away with a question in your mind about which one is right, then most likely whatever preaching caused you to have question should never be followed. Follow the type of preaching that says this is right and this is wrong. This is why preachers must preach absolutes, for God always presents absolutes in the Bible.

Years ago I had a preacher tell me that I am too black and white in my preaching and in how I lived my life. He told me if I was going to be successful, then I need to get some gray areas in my life and preaching. My response was that God never has any gray areas; all of God's areas are black or white, right or wrong.

When you are faced with a decision on whom or what to follow, always remember to follow the side that gives you an absolute that is based on the Scriptures. If a preacher leaves you with doubt about what is right and wrong in a certain area, then you must be careful about following this preacher. We must remember the Bible teaches us in Romans 14:23, *"And he that doubteth is damned if he eat, because he eateth not of faith: for whatsoever is not of faith is sin."* We all need the type of preacher who gives us absolutes. This type of preaching will certainly make more people mad, but this type of preaching will also save people from ruining their life in sin. Let's be careful about following those who leave questions. Always be sure to follow those who leave absolutes based on God's Word.

Thank God for the Word "is."

2 Timothy 3:16
"All scripture is given by inspiration of God, and is profitable for doctrine, for reproof, for correction, for instruction in righteousness:"

One thing we all have to be thankful for in this verse is the word *"is."* What a small word, but what a powerful impact it has on the Christian life.

God said, *"All scripture is given by inspiration of God..."* God wanted us to first of all understand that the Bible we have and read is inspired by God for us today. That Bible is the King James Bible 1611. Yes, It is inspired because God's Word has always been inspired. When God preserved His Word, because His words were inspired, He preserved the inspiration of those words as well.

Let me take this one step further. Not only is God's Word inspired, but we can also see that His Word is profitable to us in many areas. It is profitable to give us the doctrine to believe. It is profitable to reprove us or to convict us. It is profitable to correct us when we are doing wrong, and It is profitable to instruct us on how to live right.

Without that little word *"is"* in this verse, all of this would not be attainable today. Without the Scriptures being inspired today, then God's Word also would not be profitable to us today in the areas we have described above. Oh thank God that He included the word *"is"* in this verse.

Because God's Word is inspired today and is profitable to us today, be sure to read It as It will help you with the problems you face. Whatever the problem you are facing right now, let me remind you, God's Word is profitable to help you regarding that problem. It cannot help you with that problem if you don't read It to find out the answer to your problem. Don't get so busy that you never have time to read this wonderful

Book. At the least, spend fifteen minutes a day reading the Bible looking for that one thing that will be profitable for you today. We have a wonderful book in the Bible; let's not waste Its profitability to us by not using It and reading It.

www.ingramcontent.com/pod-product-compliance
Lightning Source LLC
LaVergne TN
LVHW051550070426
835507LV00021B/2508